GAP ODYSSEY

Navigating the Business Highway: For Young Professionals and Experienced Leaders

Mark D. Malis

authorHOUSE®

AuthorHouse™
1663 Liberty Drive, Suite 200
Bloomington, IN 47403
www.authorhouse.com
Phone: 1-800-839-8640

© 2009 Mark D. Malis. All rights reserved.

No part of this book may be reproduced, stored in a retrieval system, or transmitted by any means without the written permission of the author.

First published by AuthorHouse 10/19/2009

ISBN: 978-1-4490-2484-0 (e)
ISBN: 978-1-4490-2483-3 (sc)

Library of Congress Control Number: 2009910598

Printed in the United States of America
Bloomington, Indiana

This book is printed on acid-free paper.

To Jodi, Ryan, Sarah and Emily...the ultimate inspirations!

Gap Odyssey

Navigating the Business Highway:
For Young Professionals and Experienced Leaders

By Mark D. Malis

With Contributions by Allison Conrad

And a forward by Dr. Paul Voss

Contents

Forward · xi
Introduction · xv

Gap Odyssey – Section 1
Navigating the Business Highway - The Young & Aspiring Professional

1. What College Didn't Teach · 1
2. Creating Early Impressions · 7
3. The Art of Influence · 16
4. Clique Here · 22
5. Hit, Hold or Fold · 26
6. You're on a Mission, Not an Adventure · 32
7. Charting Your Own Course · 37
8. Where's the Bar? · 42

Gap Odyssey – Section 2
Navigating the Business Highway - The Experienced Leader

9. A Workforce Like Never Before · 49
10. It's More than Just a Great GPA and SAT Score · 55
11. Capitalize on Culture · 60
12. Communication Beyond the Four Walls · 63
13. Engagement, Commitment & Accountability · 68
14. New Chapters, New Approaches, New Aspirations · 76

Forward

Generations. A topic throughout all history.

In the pastoral comedy *As You Like It*, Shakespeare famously wrote of the "seven ages of man," those rites of passage that mark all our lives, those transitions from infancy to adolescence, to adulthood and eventually to old age. It's a poignant and moving speech. In his plays, Shakespeare often explored the transition from teen to young adult (think of Romeo and Juliet), the transition from young rebellious heir-apparent (and Prince of Wales) into the reigning monarch Henry V, and the evolution of young and single to not-so-young and married (the common trajectory found in his comedies). In short, Shakespeare found in such moments, those gaps in our lives, to be a rich source for dramatic exploration and opportunity.

Gap Odyssey—in ways quite different from Shakespeare—also examines a moment of change and transformation. In this case, the transition experienced by thousands of shocked college graduates each and every year, that recognition that the real world (however defined) plays by a different set of rules than the norms found on the college campus or in university life. The concept of "shedding the college persona" remains an integral part of professional development—a transition experienced by many young professionals.

When this new generation of college graduates enters into the workforce, they will bring with them a decidedly different life experience and skill set than the managers, directors, and seasoned professionals to whom they report. Those entering the professional world will need survival skills to navigate the tricky new currents of corporate life that at-times embody a "sink or swim" mentality.

These young professionals must learn—they must adapt to new realities and they must evolve into the expectations of professional life. It's a difficult transition (a paradigm shift of sorts) that all must experience.

But, as Sir Isaac Newton's ***Third Law*** reminds us, for every reaction there exists an equal but opposite reaction. Thus, for every adaptation and evolution required of the younger set, those established business professionals must also re-evaluate and adapt. Experienced mangers, directors, and professionals also face numerous challenges, questions, and anxieties. The old "my way or the highway" approach no longer serves as a useful, efficacious model. Consequently, many senior leaders need to make adjustments and, ironically, may often feel out of the loop or unprepared to work with this emergent population.

Gap Odyssey presents a number of key points and suggestions for dealing with "this generation like never before." Indeed, in terms of technology, the younger the individual, the farther and farther ahead of the curve they seem to be. It's almost counter-intuitive. These young professionals moved through middle school, high school, and college surrounded by a myriad of technological marvels—new innovations introduced into and throughout their lives. As a result, they both expect and (to a certain extent) need continual stimulation and novelty. Mangers need to adapt to this reality.

Charles Darwin's famous book ***On the Origin of Species*** (1859) introduced the concept of evolution to the English speaking world. In this book, Darwin stressed the link between adaptation and survival. Darwin did not speak of the survival of the strongest; if strength and strength alone mattered, the huge dinosaurs would still roam the earth. Darwin rather postulated the survival of the fittest, those organisms (or corporations) with the agility and the ability to adapt to and with the changing environments.

The history of business in the United States is full of once-vital corporations who failed to adapt, companies that remained chained to a certain way of doing business with a certain technology, serving a fixed market. Many of these corporations no longer exist. But markets, as we know, change—they move and evolve. As a result, so must companies. Naturally, so must the workforce and those managers who lead the workforce. In this new environment, managers must often make the first and most conspicuous moves.

In addition to exploring the so-called generation gap, this book also provides valuable commentary on corporate culture. Executives frequently use the word culture without precise definition or explanation. Yet corporate culture, like other types of culture, must be defined if one seeks to measure culture, and by extension, improve or enhance culture. For example, with the rapid changes in technology—we've moved from land lines, to cell phones, to e-mails, to text messages, to Facebook, and as of this writing, to Twitter, all in a very short 10-15 years. Thus, the way in which we communicate and how we choose to process information contributes to and helps define our culture. Yet one type of technology does not suit each and every business situation. How do we know when to use e-mail or when a phone call (not to mention a face-to-face visit) might be a more effective rhetorical strategy?

Gap Odyssey does not pretend to be the final word on these crucial topics. It does, however, seek to introduce young professionals and seasoned professionals to the demanding realities found in corporate America today. **Gap Odyssey** asks excellent questions and offers sage and sound advice. It will serve as a fabulous primer for those recent college grads trying to find a place in the dynamic world of business. Moreover, it offers insights into this genuine human resource for the more experienced executive. In the final analysis, **Gap Odyssey** introduces important concepts, offers practical and concrete advice, and creates a basis for moving forward with intelligence and purpose.

Gap Odyssey

INTRODUCTION

A generation is defined as "the entire body of individuals born and living at about the same time, and having similar ideas, problems, attitudes, etc". Whether ancient time, the present, or those to come, generations are always an intriguing topic of assessment and comparison.

Without going down the path of history, the present time in culture brings a unique workforce like never before. With four extremely diverse workforce categories in place, there may never be another "storm" of generations in place again, and if so, they will likely never be as divergent as today's.

With the baby boomer age still clinging to the latter stages of career livelihood, they are the last in the dying breed of the truly older era. They grew up in the nickel cinema, the advent of TV, weekend family picnics, the introduction of central air conditioning, the civil rights movement, and the tight extended family values. Weekends were spent not in front of the latest reality TV show or Wii game, but rather at the grandparents enjoying conversation over dinner and then huddling around the new medium of television watching Ed Sullivan, Wild Kingdom and the like. There were few dual-working spouses as dad arrived home each night like clockwork and mom was ready with dinner on the table. No pop-in the microwave dinners, no regular stop by's to Chick-fil-A or Chili's, no running from kids event to event. It's truly the last of the family bonding generation.

New lifestyles have brought multi-careers, multi-vehicles, expendable income, entrepreneurship, and most importantly, technology advances never imagined just years ago. The desire to regularly communicate in a face-to-face manner has been replaced with email, IM's, social networks and tweets. The days of kids laughing and screaming filling the streets are replaced by online internet game competitions and computer/phone chatter.

Each generation brings its own new advances and changes. It doesn't matter what era, things just change over time. However, think about the fact that today's current workforce has a mix of individuals that grew up in libraries and used slide rules compared to those brought up with Google searches, iPhones, and mega-powered Macbooks. It doesn't really get more extreme than that.

There has been a lot written on the topic of workplace generations, much of which highlights census data, and the wants and needs of Gen X and Gen Y. This book won't address this redundancy. Rather, as authors with over fifty years of combined senior leadership business experience, we've attempted to present a real world assessment of the generational climate, with the hope of creating some "aha" moments for both the entering business professional and experienced leader. It's our goal to **keep it real,** and to convey straight talk that benefits a diverse readership.

This writing is distinguished in two sections, expressed for the view of two audiences. Chapters 1 through 8 are for the eyes of the young and aspiring, the new generation that we reference as Gen^m (that takes the place of "Millenials"). Gen^m group members will truly redefine how business is conducted, how work is performed, how entertainment evolves, and how life is enjoyed. They will tackle head on the issues of global warming, transportation emissions, politics and terrorism, and population diversity, and will transform these issues into a new fabric of lifestyle that will radically change the world dynamic for decades to come.

In chapters 9 through 13 we provide a different vantage point, this one for the view of the experienced manager/leader. This group, chartered to lead success in a hyper-paced, fluid, and extremely competitive economic climate, now also face the challenge of incorporating a new generation spirit, eagerness and intelligence. Gen^m inclusion will require that traditional leadership methods and mindsets become reframed, creating a new dynamic (with huge near and long implications) in the evolving change management landscape.

Gap Odyssey – Section 1

Navigating the Business Highway - The Young & Aspiring Professional

Chapter 1
What College Didn't Teach

The higher education system has never been more competitive. Entrance requirements into colleges are higher, curriculums are tougher, grading tighter, and overall competition for the "best jobs" upon graduation is much steeper. In the academic sense, college students have never been better prepared. But this academic sense isn't everything however. More and more Genms are finding the transition from campus to corporate to be much more difficult than they thought it would be. And more and more seasoned executives are finding the newer entrants somewhat lacking in basic knowledge of how to look, act, and operate in the corporate environment.

Time to get off mom and dad's payroll

Senior year comes, and the race to find the "dream job" begins. Career fairs, résumé preparation, mock interviewing, cover letters, and the like become all consuming for the aspiring near-term graduate. Ultimately, jobs are secured for most, and a deep sigh of relief finally arrives. As the final semester winds down, graduation ceremonies take place, tassels are turned, apartments are emptied, and now the fun begins.

> *"More and more Gen^{m}s are finding the transition from campus to corporate to be much more difficult than they thought it would be."*

From the academic perspective the current generation is the brightest and most technologically prepared group en masse to enter the workforce. But that doesn't quite translate into immediate nor guaranteed success in the corporate landscape.

In both personal interviews and formal surveys, recent company hires from directly off the college campus highlight numerous tough transitions that they faced that ultimately "college never taught", and that may truly be the difference between success and failure in the competitive corporate landscape.

The early morning wake up call

Interestingly, one of the first challenges expressed was the pressure to get up in the morning, and get to work on time, everyday. Now for the experienced professional this likely creates a good chuckle over the morning coffee, but in the eyes of the young twenty-something old this is a genuine matter.

> *"Even with the perks of flex time and flex schedules the issue of getting to work on time on a consistent basis is a challenging event for many of the best and brightest."*

In college, you could go out any —or every — night of the week because, if you planned your semester calendar well, you could sleep off the aftereffects and potentially still get through the next day's curriculum. Online class agendas and assignments create more flexibility for actual class attendance, or at least concentration.

Fast forward to the corporate world and the young and aspiring can still party hearty. But unfortunately the alarm now rings at 6:30 a.m. It's that dreaded wake up call. Shower up, figure out those clothes (oops, not those raggedy jeans I used to wear in Psych 430), get that hair done (just right), find those darn car keys (where did I leave those the night before), and off we go. But hmm, gotta stop for that desperately needed first jolt of java, the jump-start energy bar, and life's little nuisance of gas in the tank. All good, except for that wonderful commute time to the office which is just a tad lengthier than that walk across campus to the first class of the day. And I've got to do this five days each week....what?!

 You're a freshman, again

As seniors on the college scene, there is that sense of kingpin status. But upon entry into the doors of corporate fame, the recent college hire realizes there is no such thing as entitlement anymore. That great GPA that was reflected on the resume means nothing now. In the world of corporate get ahead/stay ahead, "time to productivity" is crucial, and no-one gets the free pass. Today's successes yields tomorrow's enhanced expectations without those relaxing extensive winter, spring and summer class breaks. For the recent college hire you're back at freshman status, but now you're looking up at not the seniors, but the mega-seniors. ...enced, sometimes electric/sometimes cynical peers ar... genuinely care about you, but may also care less abou... dust.

Keen college graduates also quickly recognize that there's a bit of gap between what was actually learned in college compared to how the corporate world really operates. Now in the accounting or legal professions, as just two examples, audit, cash flow, or contract preparation work may be somewhat transferable, but even in those situations most corporate functions have differing time lines, reporting procedures, checks and balance processes, etc. that the classroom never approached.

> "All that learning in Psych, Calc, and Literature doesn't quite have that direct transfer correlation to success here in your cubicle."

Into the world of sales, human resources, customer support, system integration, and so forth, the dimensions of performance are much grayer and more fluid. Process differentiation is widespread, customer expectations individually unique, manager mentalities on wide spectrums, and the bulls-eye of success may seem like throwing a dart with a blindfold on. All that learning in Psych, Calc, and Literature doesn't quite have that direct transfer correlation to success here in your cubicle. So where was that advanced class on "adaptation to the corporate world"? Not anywhere to be found. Suddenly, you find yourself unprepared for this latest exam for the "course" called My First Job.

This is definitely different than college

Short learning curves are a constant in most corporate cultures. For the recent college hire, the days of knowing months in advance about the next mid-term or final test, and the paced ability to prep for those, is over. Competitive indexes, economic and political factors, internal strategy modifications, and fluid customer expectations all create a requirement for now-time learning, adaptability and execution. Corporate mentors and managers are great directional leads for staying focused, yet ongoing self-driven learning promotes staying ahead in the game.

A quick and easy realization upon entering the workforce for the recent college hire is that everyone is older, and typically more experienced. Routines are set, processes established, relationships nurtured, and opinions firmed. Even for the experienced new hire entering the culture with various generations entrenched, the ability to effectively acclimate, fit in, and drive early productivity and effectiveness can be daunting.

> *"Corporate mentors and managers are great directional leads for staying focused, yet ongoing self-driven learning promotes staying ahead in the game."*

Let's face it, on the college campus you'd sometimes see the "more mature" aged student, but that's typically more the exception than the norm. While differences exist in the college student age bracket, there tend to be more commonalities than differences across the spectrum. There aren't too many debates over today's pop music v. the Pips or reality TV v. Leave it to Beaver.

In the overall hierarchical scheme, age and experience create not unique, but imposing adjustments for the recent college hire that the academic rigor never addresses. The term "bright" is a relative term when contrasting that of a 22 year old v. 40 year old. And there's the additional qualifier of book-smart bright v. business savvy bright. You may be a critical hire, you may be bright on numerous dimensions, but the true reality is that you're also likely low on the proverbial totem pole to begin with, and no matter how you cut it, that's a significant change from the "personal control on my own terms" mentality on the college campus.

Welcome to the real world – try to keep up!

Entry into the workforce post-graduation also brings the realization that the corporate pace is typically quite frenetic. Deadlines shift, projects get modified, budgets get whacked, and team members get added or moved, all under the auspices of change. Accelerated technology, seamless means of communication channels, and increased customer and competitive demands combine to create fluid, hyper-paced cultures never seen in even the most distinguished corporations. The college student has never operated in such a nebulous, ever-changing climate with the stakes so high. In business, it's keep up, or quickly get lost in the shuffle.

Besides pace, organizations tend to promote that never-ending sequence of communication events called "meetings". These "productivity sessions" can range from the mundane to the strategic, but regardless of the outcome they do a great job in filling one's Outlook calendar. For the recent college hire this creates a potential maze of planning, presentation, direction and confusion based on the topic agenda, state of urgency, desired outcomes, and audience temperature. So many college hires diminish early impressions based on their inability to optimally prepare, engage, and bring effective thought process to the formal meeting forum. Dazed and glossy eyed post meeting looks just validate that this isn't quite the same as your sorority chapter meetings or student government clubs.

> *"The college student has never operated in such a nebulous, ever-changing climate with the stakes so high. In business, it's keep up, or quickly get lost in the shuffle."*

While college students deal with the semester to semester class schedules and cumulative grades, the pressure of such doesn't quite resemble that of quarter-over-quarter and year-to-year financial expectations in business, particularly within the public sector. Success may yield a warm and genuine "thank you" and congratulations, but will immediately turn into a "well, what can you do next quarter?" discussion. No rest for the weary, little time to celebrate achievements, as the quarterly scorecard is the ultimate measure. Hero this quarter, potentially the under-achiever the next. Some of which is in one's personal control, others based on team or corporate metrics. However based, the "what have you done for me lately" mentality has never been more prevalent for all concerned.

Who's the boss?

A final thought from the recent college hires focuses on the delineation of customers. At the college level, customers are the faculty, peers, and probably mom and dad who are watching over the academic experience with son or daughter. In the campus environment, you typically know (and can predict) who to impress, when, and why. But in the business setting customers come from all directions…..executives, managers, peers, subordinates, vendors, user clients, and support teams. And each customer segment can become fickle at times, creating that queasy look similar to the 3-day old pizza consumption that just doesn't sit well.

But alas, it does get better….over time!

Thought Question: You start working for a company out of college. Your manager is an "early bird" in that he likes to promptly hold 7:30am update briefings with his entire team each Monday morning. His expectation is that each of his staff will provide a summary of the prior weeks' activities, and overview for the coming week. What things should you do to best come across in these weekly sessions?

Chapter 1 Highlights

For the college hire entering the workforce, there is no such thing as entitlement anymore.

In the world of corporate get ahead/stay ahead, "time to productivity" is crucial, and no-one gets the free pass.

The bulls-eye of success may seem like throwing a dart with a blindfold on.

For the new hire, the ability to effectively acclimate, fit in, and drive early productivity and effectiveness can be daunting.

Accelerated technology, seamless means of communication channels, and increased customer and competitive demands combine to create fluid, hyper-paced cultures never seen before.

In business, it's keep up, or quickly get lost in the shuffle.

Chapter 2
Creating Early Impressions

College graduates today are well-steeped in everything from global affairs to the latest social networking phenomenon. Since the day they were born, they have been included, involved, and incorporated by everyone in their surroundings. First there is doting attention from their parents, then persistent attention from every large consumer product and services company which markets directly to them – their way. But upon entrance to the business world, suddenly the focus isn't on catering to the twenty-something individual, but how well the individual can assimilate and fit in. Creating a great first impression is the initial crucial challenge in this matter.

Getting started

You've got your company issued laptop, secured your building access ID card, attended the half-day "welcome to our great company" orientation program, and most importantly, secured that cube space by some windows (or at least by the good-looking colleague nearby). Stapler, check.... file folders, got 'em....binder clips, absolutely (in all the great sizes and colors)....and post-it notes, you betcha. And it's pretty cool to see your name on those new company business cards!

You're ready to go to launch that career, but quickly realize that being the freshman (again) is quite different on the corporate v. college campus. You want to make your mark, get recognized, climb that ladder of success, but reality promptly smacks you head on reinforcing that you're the fresh new face who's a bit starry-eyed by the magnitude of the business pace and complexity.

Brand Y-O-U

Creating impacting early impressions requires a bit of shedding that college persona. Young and cute is great as that tends to get associated with energy, creativity, and boundless exuberance. There's no major baggage or ingrained bad habits that typically comes with age and redundancy. But youth also brings an internal perception of being inexperienced and naïve. You're not quite that "go to" person, just yet.

But with fresh ideas and that will-to-succeed, the cliché "the world is your oyster" is no more evident, but it's about seizing the opportunity. Shedding that college persona and creating impacting early impressions ties to the concept of creating your own personal brand. While early in one's career, every engagement creates a perception opportunity. So how do you want to be perceived? A simple list of probing questions should hopefully create some personal introspection on your own personal brand.

- What kind of image do others have of me?
- What kind of image do I project?
- Am I reliable or do I over-promise and under-deliver in my commitments?
- Do I show respect for others?
- Am I trustworthy in my dealings with others?
- Am I punctual?
- Do I listen to what others have to say?
- Am I a team player?
- How is my background unique?
- What natural talents do I have that will make me better than most at this job?
- Over the next year (and 3 years), how do I want to be perceived by the people who matter most within the company?

This list can extend well beyond these initial questions, but creates a starting point for "who you are" in the eyes of many, most importantly, yourself.

Mirror, mirror on the wall

So let's get started with discussing how to make impacting early impressions, and begin with the topic of dress/attire. The "dress for success" mantra isn't about wearing that high priced outfit with all the right accessories, but rather is about meshing properly into your corporate environment, however that looks. Whether it's a jeans culture v. business casual or professional attire, it's critical to "look the part". While being individual and unique may work in the social setting, in the business world it's about blending in. Be observant, and follow the lead of others. How do the highly successful in your company look? While appearance certainly isn't the only ingredient to success, the way you package yourself does make a difference.

> *"The "dress for success" mantra isn't about wearing that high priced outfit with all the right accessories, but rather is about meshing properly into your corporate environment, however that looks."*

The physical package also extends beyond the clothes being worn. Look in the mirror. What does your hairstyle and makeup convey? Polished and professional, or out there and a bit radical? And what about that pierced nose or tongue? Is that the packaging image you see among the best and brightest in your work environment? So many early impressions that people make occur before you even make that first presentation or attend that initial meeting. It's no different than the impressions we make at parties or the first few days of class. Who do we want to hang around with, talk to, or sit next to? Those decisions are typically made on appearance factors alone since no gauge has yet been established on any other dimension. Whether the early stage worker accepts it or not, this is a crucial aspect of initial impacting impressions.

In Chapter 1 we referenced consistently getting to work on time as a dilemma expressed from many recent college hires. That topic won't be drawn out here again, but suffice to say that managers, peers and executives do notice those aspiring individuals that arrive on time (or early) v. those that habitually show up late (and likely looking a bit disheveled). Highlighted in a challenging economic period, people notice those individuals who step up and invest more work hours to help the company succeed. So set that alarm to go off an extra 30 or 60 minutes earlier in the morning, and create an easy positive work ethic impression.

Make good use of all those research skills

Some early impacting impressions can be made by just knowing the business, industry sector, competitive landscape, and so forth. What better way to come across well than by knowing the space you're working in, and having intelligence come from your verbal and written interactions.

> "*Learning is so critical, so invest the time to scour your company website, learn your company products and services (even if this isn't in your realm of responsibility), and understand your company's customer base and competition.*"

Typical initial orientations are really geared to provide a surface overview of the company history, products/services, benefit offerings, and other such information. It doesn't significantly extend down from the 30,000 foot level. Learning is so critical, so invest the time to scour your company website, learn your company products and services (even if this isn't in your realm of responsibility), and understand your company's customer base and competition. Reading industry articles, subscribing to (and actually reading) market periodicals, joining and attending industry associations, and connecting within online networks are just some ways to jump-start this effort. Have you read and analyzed your company annual report and quarterly updates? And have you compared and contrasted those against those of your primary and secondary competitors? The initiative to gain knowledge outside a formal internal program will create big dividends in how you are perceived by others, and the confidence you'll bring to the table.

A positive attitude is worth its weight in gold

Attitude is always an easy-read for managers and executives. Do you have a can-do approach to work, and are you one of the first to volunteer for additional new projects? Or do you come across as whiny and complaining? Do you charge forth and bust through potential landmines? Or do you project that everyone is out to get you, and that the world just sucks? Do you stay focused on business, and the task at hand? Or do you bring every personal problem and crisis into the workplace?

Attitude is an easy dimension to control, and rest assured your management team makes a quick (and ongoing) assessment of you on this dimension. Want to get labeled early on as a malcontent? Well, just show up late, hide at work, and ignore those around you. Conversely, bring that smile, energy, and initiative to the workplace, and you're well on your way towards continued positive impressions made of you. Even if project or assignment results don't always hit the home-run, great attitude will always be measured in the equation called effort.

Flip on that light bulb over your head

Attitude also leverages into thinking of new, creative work to do, and projecting that as additional impact initiatives. One of the greatest compliments I received in my career was when a CEO I reported to stated that he truly respected me because "I would stay up at night thinking about ways to make the company better". Now this doesn't mean that I didn't get adequate sleep, nor is the comment distinguishable for just the senior level role. And it doesn't mean that work should be all-consuming, because work-life success needs to be balanced. Rather, every employee has the opportunity to bring fresh, thought provoking and impactful ideas to their respective company. The job isn't nine to five, and really hasn't been for some time. So whether it's on the commute meter, or relaxing back at the home front, keep a note pad handy to capture those random thoughts and ideas.

- Can they make a difference within your business, and for whom?
- What's the cost and timeline to execute, and what additional resources are necessary?
- Does this fit within the overall business strategy, or is it just "out there"?
- What's the incremental revenue opportunity?
- How will our customers (internal and external) react?

These are just some basic questions to consider when contemplating new thoughts. The key though is not to be bashful when you have a great idea. History cites example after example of business success stories that started in the entrepreneur's garage, or were detailed out on a restaurant napkin. Formality is not the issue, it's the initiative to try that counts, and the attitude that's conveyed when making your pitch.

> *"History cites example after example of business success stories that started in the entrepreneur's garage, or was detailed out on a restaurant napkin. "*

Communication is the key, the core ingredient, the big kahuna

So far we've addressed image, attitude and research as some of the dimensions around early impacting impressions, and shedding a bit of that college persona. But there's certainly more to it than just that.

To complete the package, effective communication and presentation skills are "a must" in effectively launching (and building upon) your career.

BTW, written communication skills R important 2

Communication skills are demonstrated on both the written and verbal side. The college student is accustomed in dealing with abbreviations. TTFN, LOL, BRB, OMG have all become part of the text and email messaging vernacular, and not just in the world of the teenager and college student. It's a part of our overall daily communication embraced by the mass generations. While the world of abbreviations works well in the time sensitive social networking arena where brevity is preferred, in the business context there's still a sense of formality and properness that is required (at least in most business cultures). It's still unwise for a recent college hire to email their manager (who likely represents another generation set) with OMG somewhere in the messaging. It may work with your BFF, but probably not with the big-boss Bob.

That same big-boss would also like to see correspondences that show proper spelling and grammar, and reflect clear and thorough thought processes. In communications, nothing irks managers more than poorly written messaging. Yes, Word software has spelling and grammar check, but it won't catch everything, and it sure won't catch the intent of messages! So, within your messaging:

- What are you truly trying to convey?
- Have you got your facts straight?
- Have you done your homework?
- Who is your target audience?
- Does your message flow effectively?
- What are your desired outcomes?

Remember that every engagement, whether live or within email/voicemail is an impression opportunity. People (whether an internal or external customer) may not always remember the great messaging you do, but they probably can recall the poor ones.

For critical messaging, develop either a mental or written outline/roadmap that sequences what you want to convey, when and how. Inject complete thoughts v. simple short sentences. Read, and then re-read your drafted message (before clicking on that dreaded "send" button) to ensure you're articulating exactly what you want to get across.

Beep. Leave a message

The same key points apply to voicemail. Many individuals make critical errors in judgment, and ultimately shoot themselves in the foot, based on miscues on voicemail. Don't ramble, don't be too cute or humorous, and don't call from that loud bar. Particularly for important voicemail messages, create that mental/written outline, think about what you want to convey and the audience in which you're communicating to, and then succinctly get your message across. Most managers despise long voicemail messages, so remember the aspect of brevity. Keep it short and simple.

For either voicemail, email, text messaging, etc, remember that each mode is a trail that can last forever. That applies not only to your direct target audience, but as we know messaging in all forms can be forwarded to others that get referred to as message strings. With that, now you may have a whole new extended audience that may or may not know you, may not understand your style of communication, but nonetheless has an impression opportunity of you. So take your time and make sure you're coming across the way you desire.

Can you speak to groups? And we don't mean through Twitter

A similar approach applies to the art of formal presentation skills. The goal of presenting is not to read off index cards or conduct the way-too-often "death by PowerPoint". As with the other forms of communication, effective presentations are about knowing your subject matter, recognizing who your audience is, and identifying what you are seeking to convey and achieve as an outcome. Don't get cute with new PowerPoint templates that are not the company norm, inappropriately injecting comics, or inserting pictures that may be deemed as questionable. In most successful presentations, it's about engaging and connecting with the audience, and not reading directly off the PowerPoint slide (nothing insults an audience participant more than a presenter who just reads off slides). By engaging the audience, a dialogue is created, information flows more seamlessly, and non-verbal cues are more easily recognizable. Most importantly, presenters should practice their delivery ahead of time to evaluate the intended content, ensure time allotments are maintained, and have the opportunity to make any last minute adjustments.

While more spontaneous, general meetings also provide an opportunity for impression making. Do you prepare for a meeting in advance (when possible)? Do you come prepared to take notes? Do you establish eye contact with the other participants when they speak? Do you actively participate where possible, and convey professional thoughts in an articulated fashion? And remember the landmine of bringing the cell phone/Blackberry to the meeting, and getting distracted or engaged in a text message stream with your buddies. Your colleagues and managers in the audience will notice.

You don't have to be alone

Up to this point we've highlighted the impressions made by appearance/image, learning, attitude, and communication. It's a hefty task to master all of these dimensions, and many of the most seasoned professionals struggle as well with some of these. A resource to help aid in the skill building of these required dimensions is that of a mentor in your organization or community. A mentor is typically a more senior individual that volunteers their time to help in the development of an understudy. Mentors can be huge sounding boards, practice partners, and overall champions for your cause. By finding the right mentor (one who takes the relationship seriously and invests the proper time) you'll likely have that advocate that will help you achieve that climb to the peaks of success.

Thought Question: You happen to run into your company CEO for the first time in the break room. He introduces himself to you, and asks who you are. With only a small window of time (let's say 60 seconds), what would you want to state about yourself?

Chapter 2 Highlights

Shedding that college persona and creating impacting early impressions ties to the concept of creating your own personal brand.

Every engagement creates a perception opportunity.

While appearance certainly isn't the only ingredient to success, the way you package yourself does make a difference.

Learning is so critical, so invest the time to scour your company website, learn your company products and services (even if this isn't in your realm of responsibility), and understand your company's customer base and competition.

The initiative to gain knowledge outside a formal internal program will create big dividends in how you are perceived by others, and the confidence you'll bring to the table.

Great attitude will always be measured in the equation called effort.

Mentors can be huge sounding boards, practice partners, and overall champions that will help you achieve that climb to the peaks of success.

Chapter 3
The Art of Influence

Influence is a true art. It's an act or process of leading other individuals to a shared solution for an issue, task or problem. The term varies from the simplistic to the complex and can engage either a small set or large group of participants. Authority and level within a company will naturally enable a certain amount of influence. For the recent college hire it can be a bit more challenging in determining how best to influence without perceived authority. Whatever the case, influence is a key required competency for success in the business world.

Mergers and acquisitions, new product strategies and corporate realignments all require some levels of influence to get the job accomplished. Some efforts may be subtle; others may be direct or darn right hostile.

> *"Whatever the landscape, influencing skills are a must."*

Influencing starts at an early age

When the young toddler, even before the early development of verbal skills, coos at mom, dad, or grandma, tugs at their shirt, or snuggles when they want something, they're using early influence skills to achieve a desired outcome. And in most cases this works quite effectively.

In the story Tom Sawyer, Tom was tasked by Aunt Polly to paint the picket fence. Quickly realizing that the task-at-hand was too physically demanding, and well outside the scope of fun, Tom influenced his neighborhood pals to see the task in a different light, and to actually pay to participate in the chore. Ultimately Tom influenced a small crew to paint his picket fence while he rested under the shady tree with a ripe apple, supervising the efforts, and marveling at his payments from the merry band.

By the teen years kids influence, barter and negotiate on all fronts relative to the latest technology toys, who's accepted into what clique, and which classmate to date.

Take influence from the home front to the business front

It's no wonder then that when individuals hit the post-college corporate world most are semi-masters of influence. But there are still nuances and techniques to learn. Looking to enhance or leverage your reputation with others in your business? How about meeting that new "rising or super star" in the organization to frame a new network contact? Seeking to get new resources relative to additional people staffs, enhanced technologies, or increased budget allocations? How about making that next profitable deal either at the internal, external customer or acquisition level? Whatever the landscape, influencing skills are a must.

In its basic form, three key questions tend to frame influence:

- What are you looking to accomplish?
- Who is the audience to be influenced?
- What influence tactics should optimally be used?

Relationship influence v. tangible influence may take distinct and different skills for success, but in either scenario a primary tenet is that the manner in which information is presented is often just (if not more) important as the content of the influence.

> *"Influence is a true art."*

The personal approach

So just how do you most effectively influence? In the somewhat basic element, individuals attempt to influence others by simply getting them to like you. That nice smile (showing off all that great prior orthodontia work), exchanging pleasantries over time, sharing similar college stories or rooting for the same alma mater, or growing up in the same area can all lend to an easy open door for influence. If you "like me", perhaps I can get you to do something for me. This "personal appeal" approach is no doubt the form of influence most prevalent throughout the ages of time.

> "If you "like me", perhaps I can get you to do something for me. This "personal appeal" approach is no doubt the form of influence most prevalent throughout the ages of time."

If a + b = c, then clearly a = c − b

Utilizing reason and logic is an additional tactic to influence. Got your facts straight? Do they make a compelling argument or case? Does it all appear nicely sound, tidy, and logical? If so, it's hard for someone to dispute a particular course of action or path to take when logic and reason exists. These two elements are used frequently in business proposals and strategy sessions because they drive a perception of credibility for the influencer. When all aligns right with reason and logic, the audience tends to think that the influencer "knows his/her stuff", believes it creates a compelling argument for success and typically refrains from going against the grain of momentum that logic and reason can bring.

You are so suave

Getting someone in a good mood in advance of influencing is yet another approach that can tend to yield positive outcomes. Doing someone an advance favor, highlighting a current or recent success or win, paying a particular compliment or even telling a good joke can create a wonderful stage for "what's to come" in influencing. It's like the teenager who compliments mom on how she looks (when does that ever occur) before asking for $30 bucks for the movie and dinner night out with friends. Catch the right mood, pay the right compliments and you pave the way for potential good things to happen. The key in "mood" development is not coming across so obvious that your intentions become quickly apparent, are dismissed or are viewed with suspect. As such, the "good mood" tactic should be approached with caution based on this potential double-edge outcome.

Let's make a deal

Trading favors may also work effectively. This is probably most utilized in the political arena as legislative votes many times get secured through the exchange of favors, or injection of "pork" to help a certain cause or geographic area. In the business world, the motives aren't quite as blatant, but the mentality of one hand washing the other still exists. "Do me this favor, and I'll remember that the next time you might need something" occurs either directly or subtly in corporate America. While trading favors can have genuine and positive relationship and action outcomes, the risk in today's world of skepticism is that outward or behind the scenes favor trading tends to be viewed as suspect. Additionally, when a favor (or series of favors) is extended, one never knows when that scorecard will be asked to become balanced, and under what terms and conditions. Therefore, this is another tactic that bears caution.

Tug at the heartstrings a little

Back on the more upbeat side, you can exert influence by appealing to other's emotions, ideals, and values. As an example, I'm always a pushover and enthusiastic customer for every Girl Scout who takes the time to walk the neighborhood, ring the doorbell, and pitch her mint or shortbread cookies. Girl scouts just have this attached association of "what's good" in America, so what's another box or two (or ten) of cookies that will likely make their way to the office break room anyway. Business executives (and politicians, boy do they) consistently play to the values and emotions of their constituents. Most of it's done in a positive framework, with somewhat sincere intentions to rally together for a positive cause. New medical or drug research and technology development advancements, as business examples, are typically aligned to our customer's emotions, ideals and values.

Get support for your cause

Certainly the forming of coalitions can also exert influence. Creating effective coalitions requires the ability to identify individuals in the organization who may have similar interests and motives. This resulting power-of-many can truly sway the direction for many key decisions on the business playing field. The formation of alliances that will band together to apply collective insight, buy-in and perhaps pressure is regularly seen as normal team dynamics in the business landscape. While corporate coalitions can sometimes be viewed as dark-alley politics, the establishment of effective coalitions can eliminate lengthy decision making logjams, cut through or minimize red tape, and effectively identify and eliminate potential landmines or roadblocks to success. The key to coalitions is knowing who to approach (and who to trust) within a potential formation, on what matters will the coalition exist, and to what price is incurred relative to future reciprocity.

Make them part of the solution

Lastly, getting others to participate in decision making and change takes on a consultative spin to influencing. If others feel they are part of the process, and have a say in the matters, then influence can be achieved through the shear means of healthy dialogue, interaction, and respect of opinions. If a meeting facilitator probes participants for input and feedback to a particular agenda, and seeks each members buy-in or alignment as part of the process, it ultimately becomes difficult for everyone not to fall in line with the desired outcome. There's a bit of an art to this meeting facilitation, but those that can master the technique can truly yield seamless success that creates strong acceptance and support from participants.

> *"The key to coalitions is knowing who to approach (and who to trust) within a potential formation, on what matters will the coalition exist, and to what price is incurred relative to future reciprocity."*

Who's sitting in your audience?

As we've seen, there are many means to influence. Some pretty easy, some complex. Some based on positive interests and motives, others that incorporate varying degrees of risk. But regardless of the influence strategy, knowing the audience is mission critical. Those typical business audiences will include your peers, managers, and other business unit/department contacts.

When considering the audience, ask yourself…

- Do I know who my allies are?
- Do I understand my audience's "world"?
- Am I clear on what I am seeking to accomplish?
- What are the valued interests or "currencies" of the audience?
- Have many (and particularly who) needs to buy-in?
- What is in the best interest of the organization/audience v. myself?

By successfully understanding your audience you can then best identify an influence strategy that will allow you to…

- Connect emotionally
- Establish credibility
- Frame goals and interests within common ground
- Effectively state and reinforce your desired target information
- Achieve your desired outcomes

***Thought Question:** If you have a product, service or idea that has both strengths and weaknesses, when should you present the weaknesses? Early or later in your presentation?*

CHAPTER 3 HIGHLIGHTS

Influencing is a learning and negotiation process for leading other individuals to a shared solution to an issue, task or problem.

Influence is a true art.

Relationship influence v. tangible influence may take distinct and different skills for success, but in either scenario a primary tenet is that the manner in which information is presented is often just (if not more) important as the content of the influence.

Regardless of the influence strategy, knowing the audience is mission critical.

Some influence initiatives may be subtle; others may be direct or darn right hostile.

Chapter 4
Clique Here

Measured by insider or outsider status, cliques form on just about every front within civilization. The school, the community, the club, the bar, the political landscape, the office, whatever the setting there are likely noticeable and exclusive groups of people formed together by a common bond, interest or motivation.

In the corporate culture, cliques are in abundance. Cliques can have a healthy, beneficial value. Groups or peer-sets can help you with your transition into the company, or help you through a life event like moving or becoming a spouse or a parent. Cliques can even come together to help solve workplace issues. But watch out. Associations with the cliques of gossipers, complainers, or those that exert minimal effort can be detrimental to the perception of you by key workplace leaders. Just clique wisely.

We clique all the time

The "in" crowd, the "outside crowd"; the group that exercises together versus the lumpy mid-sections that don't; the neighbors that empty the keg while rooting for their past-prime football alma mater versus the conservative middle aged folks behind the lawn mower; the team of corporate athletes on the softball field versus those just rooting in the stands.

> *"Some may claim that these are just simple groups of individuals with like interests, not cliques. But just attempt to lodge into these groups outside the associated primary and common bond and you quickly understand the dynamics of cliques. "*

In early childhood and in the simplest form they are called "play groups". Typically these are good intentioned moms getting a small group of drooling hyper-active tots together regularly for the purpose of child bonding, but more importantly adult group babysitting. If another diaper-dandy and mom attempts to inject into the play group forum, the existing group assessment takes place. Will junior play well with the group? Will this mom gossip along with us, and bring new neighborhood info tidbits with her? Will her car fit the rest of the playgroup in the event the existing moms need to bail at the last minute for that impromptu tennis game? Ah, the dilemma of inclusion.

Fast forward just a couple years and at every level of school cliques abound. The popular group, geek group, smoking/drug group, sexually active group, body piercing group, athletic group, brainy group, teacher's pet group…the list goes on and on. Some may claim that these are just simple groups of individuals with like interests, not cliques. But just attempt to lodge into these groups outside the associated primary and common bond and you quickly understand the dynamics of cliques.

Work cliques

The same can typically be said in the corporate community. Astute individuals can sense and observe the differing cliques of executives, the lunch table grabbing set of young professionals (who all tend to look the same, don't they), or the rah-rah mixed bowling league participants. Typically these cliques are positive in nature, but when the experience tends to feel like a really bad flashback to high school, it's time for a participation reassessment.

Much has been written over the years on the detriments of cliques. Too much counter-productive gossiping, narrow view sharing, behind the scenes competitiveness, jockeying for position, and overall backstabbing. All true enough in some instances. The keen corporate observer will look at certain clique dynamics and just know that the definition of "good" isn't happening.

Right cliques

While some recent research suggests a preponderance of perceived cliques in the workplace, and with the vast majority viewed as negative, there are many opportunities for constructive engagement and value to both the participants and organization. Cliques can be positive support groups within the workplace. Participants can encourage clique members to succeed, inspire members to achieve a team project, or help brainstorm ideas in which to overcome barriers to success. This collective mass, termed the collaboration clique, can truly be helpful in driving confidence and productivity. When framed effectively, such as understanding the clique ground rules and overall common bond/purpose, individual members can self-monitor the activity to maintain a productive, healthy focus and interaction.

> *"Cliques can be positive support groups within the workplace."*

"Stimulus" cliques tend to focus on attracting the "go getters" of the organization, those aspiring individuals who want to help take each other to the next level of skill, knowledge and influence in which to further impact the organization and their careers.

Social cliques can also be healthy to the essence of the culture. Like-minded members can become highly valuable support groups for dealing with personal changes in life (e.g. – becoming engaged or moving to a new apartment), adjusting to new independence from the college campus, or dealing with direct issues within the workplace (a disengaged boss, getting to work on time, rumors of downsizing, etc).

Wrong cliques

As with most aspects of the workplace, and as mentioned in a prior chapter, every engagement is a perception opportunity, and every perception counts. Clique association can be a safe and comfortable environment for its members. However, understanding the need and ability to diversify one's interactions, lunch partners, learning funnels, etc. can work to minimize the reputation as a singular or multi clique inclusion that may or may not be viewed as constructive at either the individual or team level.

Similar to other modes of professional or social networking, such as MySpace or Facebook, cliques can be very effective if you refrain from:

- Idle gossip
- Clique member exclusivity
- Excessive competitiveness
- Activity counterproductive to the company goals and values
- Primary reputation as a clique(s) member/stimulus
- Dissemination of private, classified or protected information

Finding peers and colleagues that share common goals and interests can be a great way to acclimate, learn and thrive within the business culture. Pursue those with the right spirit, openness and purpose, and cliques can be a valuable outlet for success.

Thought Question: You're part of a group clique of young professionals at work, and the group tends to have lunch together pretty regularly. All is well relative to a constructive and fun atmosphere until one of the "regulars" starts venting on her manager, who she's having some difficulty with. She's stressed and unhappy over the situation and the clique is feeling a change in group dynamic. What should you or the group do?

CHAPTER 4 HIGHLIGHTS

Cliques form on just about every front within civilization.

When the clique experience tends to feel like a really bad flashback to high school it's time for a participation reassessment.

The keen corporate observer will look at certain clique dynamics and just know that the definition of "good" isn't happening.

Cliques can be positive support groups within the workplace.

Chapter 5
Hit, Hold or Fold

The stakes are raised. You're the young college hire, eager to impress; ready to make your mark; aspiring to conquer the world. After all that study time invested in college, it's time to finally separate from the parent umbilical cord, make some money and enjoy living in the "real world".

Such great aspirations. But what becomes apparent to those with eyes open is that the corporate setting is extremely more complex than the campus setting, and competition strikes from all directions. Knowing the right move is suddenly a lot more confusing than you thought it'd be. There's no textbook or Google search result telling you how to navigate the political landscape, when/how the corporate buzzwords change (and they do – often), or how to manage that huge project you were just given.

> *"Knowing the right move is suddenly a lot more confusing than you thought it'd be."*

This isn't similar to the brainy kid in Calc III that stood out in the classroom, and that you knew would blow out the grade curve, and therefore force your study habits to increase just that much more to keep up. Nor is it like trying to make a positive impression on that hot volleyball chick - the long-legged girl that you've been dreaming about for months, but haven't had the courage to spark a conversation with because the starting football tailback has her reeling already.

Now that I am here, what do I do?

Nope, this world is indeed more complex. Dress code standards, long work hours (including all those aforementioned early wake ups), firm project deadlines, non-stop emails, and meetings, meetings, and more meetings. On top of that, this isn't revolving around a composite peer group that mainly looks similar to you. In this world there are colleagues, peers, managers, and a whole host of direct/indirect contacts that are older, with more tenure, with more overall experience, with more business savvy, and more cultural aptitude.

These are folks with knowledge of the buried landmines, awareness of the political landscape, in-the-know of who's the rising star v. the one treading water, and who's aligned to whom. They know how to "play the game", how to cover their tracks, and how to suck up when the time is appropriate.

In this complexity actions resemble chess moves with one decision impacting the chain that follows. One step forward, a couple back, and maneuvers to the side are all part of the game. In the corporate culture many players bring their thimbles or top hat to the game, and engage at varying paces with/without observance to the actual rules of the game (some of which are made along the way).

Consider your options

With multiple decision steps in the game of interaction, the choices are either to:

- Hit
- Hold, or
- Fold

All of which can be entirely right moves – or entirely wrong moves – depending on the situation.

In "hit", the player takes the initiative to take hold of situations despite the potential obstacles of experience, seniority, team dynamics, and the like. For example, a project is assigned by the manager, and the team is comprised of a diverse group with varying skill sets. It's an opportunity to stand in the forefront by exhibiting a creative, fresh spark to the initiative that can generate new perspectives to a game plan and an energy that invigorates the dynamics of the group. Being bold to step up, capture credibility, and lead through confidence and conviction can do wonders to accelerate one's status and to quickly be viewed as a high potential individual.

In "hold" mode, the approach is neither to take charge nor fold the tent, but rather to find comfortable ground to learn from experiences. It's recognizing that within either an individual or team dynamic that there are differing perspectives normally created within a diverse workforce experience. Effort is made to respect the diversity, with the ultimate goal of being part of the solution, and not the problem. The take-aways from careful observation and absorption of others' styles and approaches yield options in creating one's own brand targeted to subsequent relationship opportunities.

In "fold", feelings exist that the work dynamic may just be overwhelming and ripe in political risk, and that in the majority of scenarios experience trumps all else. The end result really isn't giving in, but rather recognizing that the challenges faced require steep learning at the present state. Others around you create the pulse and pace, and your role is to learn, observe and digest, and ultimately not get in the way. Similar to an apprenticeship type role, the young player learns from the "game master" before stepping into their own comfort light over time.

The decision to hit, hold or fold, at face value, is not easy. There are risks, upsides and consequences (both potentially positive and negative) in the ultimate direction. As mentioned earlier, business engagements yield ongoing perceptions, so there are short and long term implications in deciding what path to take.

> *"Being bold to step up, capture credibility, and lead through confidence and conviction can do wonders to accelerate one's status and to quickly be viewed as a high potential individual."*

Make your move

When assessing hit, hold or fold options within the playing field, there are a number of questions to internally reflect on:

- What am I looking to gain from the experience?
- What does success look like for both me and others around me?
- What are the barriers to success?
- Where can potential alliances be forged?
- Who are potential saboteurs?

- Do I have a basis of knowledge to make an impact?
- Is the experience a learning, observation or step-out opportunity?
- What is the political temperature?

These are all difficult assessments, and require astute skills to sort through the environment, culture and background "noise". There's a lot to be said for these internal idiosyncrasies, because these tend to be factors that aren't always obvious.

Are leaders easily detectable? Are the rules of engagement established by few or many, and are they clear to the masses? Are the meek and/or dissenters quickly dismissed, essentially told to take their game pieces and step to the side?

On this field the obvious isn't always obvious. Similar to the thrill rides of the inside and darkened roller coasters, the passenger next to you may be an ally or a foe, every sharp turn yields a new twist or rule, and every steep dip challenges the intestinal fortitude to proceed on, or sweat the bullets with eagerness for the ride to end.

> *"To the relatively inexperienced, a hit, hold or fold situation will create long-lasting lessons learned regardless of the outcome."*

But by adequately thinking through the questions posed above, the participant will begin framing their own playing field, with the boundaries and rules more clearly established and manageable. There may still be dips and curves, but ultimately they can be better predicted and controlled within the view of game architect.

Get ready to shuffle and deal again

Overall, the thrill rides that occur within organizations can be striking. Who's aligned with who and what agenda (apparent or hidden) prevails from within the culture can create interesting and sometimes troubling dynamics playing havoc on whether to hit, hold or fold.

To the relative inexperienced, a hit, hold or fold situation will create long-lasting lessons learned regardless of the outcome. For the successful conclusion, it reinforces the courage and boldness to take a chance, step out, and make a great outcome happen. For the opposite extreme, nothing is more educational than running into dysfunctional internal corporate behaviors and actions that sets everyone in their place, and crushes aspirations of creativity and equal engagement. Wounds will heal, setbacks will be analyzed (over and over again), and new game plans and strategies will be crafted to deal with the next group episode.

Thought Question: You're part of a staff meeting that's discussing new process improvement ideas. You can tell that the conversation is being dominated by the more senior level team members, and that the discussion has generated a lot of emotion and enthusiasm by those participants. From the points made you feel you might have a new idea that utilizes some Web 2.0 solutions that could help generate quicker and more efficient results, but you know that the elder staff are not up to speed on these technologies. What would you do?

Chapter 5 Highlights

In "hit", the player takes the initiative to take hold of situations despite the potential obstacles of experience, seniority, team dynamics, and the like.

"Hit" is an opportunity to stand in the forefront by exhibiting a creative, fresh spark to the initiative that can generate new perspectives to a game plan and an energy that invigorates the dynamics of the group.

In "hold" mode, the approach is neither to take charge nor fold the tent, but rather to find comfortable ground to learn from experiences.

In "fold", feelings exist that the work dynamic may just be overwhelming and ripe in political risk, and that in the majority of scenarios experience trumps all else. The end result really isn't giving in, but rather recognizing that the challenges faced require steep learning at the present state.

The decision to hit, hold or fold, at face value, is not easy. There are risks, upsides and consequences (both potentially positive and negative) in the ultimate direction.

To the relative inexperienced hit, hold or fold situations will create long-lasting lessons learned regardless of outcome. For the successful conclusion, it reinforces the courage and boldness to take a chance, step out, and make a great outcome happen.

Chapter 6
You're on a Mission, Not an Adventure

Today's new hires expect an adventure. The worldwide media reach and real-time news culture that surrounded their upbringing has put them in touch with the global community. Unlike previous generations, this group feels very connected to people in far off lands with very different backgrounds and ways of viewing the world. They've seen both the young and old influence global economies and humanitarian issues often in "real time" from their family living room. Their depth of awareness is only enhanced by the connectedness they experience online. They have a feeling of power over not only their own life, but of the lives of people in general. The world is their oyster. They can change it. It's an amazing adventure to begin life off-campus. At a macro-level this bodes well for the future. This generation fully expects to clean-up the mess of those who came before them.

How can they have the adventure and still contribute to the company bottom line? How can they keep the passion and still fit into a structured environment? How can they keep a world view and still survive their cubical years? These questions are much more prevalent now than ever before.

> "At the highest level new hires must connect to the company's purpose. Finding the personal mission in the company purpose can lead to the adventure of a lifetime- or at least a very successful career."

You've got to dive in at some point

The "first real job" is a major milestone for any college graduate in any era, but it can be an even more significant milestone for today's new hire. For some it's the payoff for a very long process that may have started with parental efforts to get into the "right preschool." For some it's a right of passage from dependence to independence. For all it represents a long awaited opportunity to impact the world around them in a way they couldn't before—as a full fledged adult.

For a surprising number the "first real job" may actually be the first job of any type. Studies have shown that while a growing number of college applicants have climbed Mount Kilimanjaro and worked in humanitarian efforts oversees during their high school breaks to enhance their resume, fewer of them have engaged in traditional, local part-time jobs. In an overscheduled upbringing dominated by organized sports, organized socializing (starting with the now common "play date,") and organized philanthropy, who has time? Gen^{m}s entering the workforce are a part of a very savvy group. When entering the workforce, there is no doubt they bring with them that unbridled confidence and broad perspective.

Making a difference

Impacting the world as an adult can seem like the beginning of an amazing adventure. Finally, all the preparation and studying is paying off. However, entering the entry-level position can be a rude awakening. While counseling a Gen^m struggling with a summer job, I was asked, "Why don't they come to me for more advice? I can really change this place. I thought I would be able to make a big impact on the business, but they just want me to do one thing- run reports and provide a summary interpretation of the same weekly data." Now, for previous generations I suspect this summer job orchestrated by this Gen^{m}s CEO father would be a great opportunity to put a good company name on the resume. However, she felt very frustrated by the gap in expectations. This was the beginning of her post-undergraduate career, her opportunity to make a significant impact, yet to her it seemed a narrow use of her talents and knowledge.

> *"Why don't they come to me for more advice? I can really change this place."*

At the highest level new hires must connect to the company's purpose, defined typically as a set of values that defines an organization and inspires and motivates its employees. It's highly likely that you will not see "purpose" listed in any company literature — not even in human resource oriented documents. Determining a true sense of company purpose can only come from interaction with a cross-section of the people within an organization. As new graduates explore opportunities within a set of potential employers, it's important to ask both management and potential peers questions around the "bigger picture" of the company purpose:

- What is the inspiration behind this company?
- What values do all employees have in common?
- What is the core set of ideas that drive innovation?

The effort required to determine a company's purpose can be invaluable when deciding whether or not a company is a "fit." Like many important decisions in life, when it's right for you, you just know it.

> *"At the highest level new hires must connect to the company's purpose."*

Bring your compass

On a day-to-day basis, each new hire should find the personal adventure in their company's strategic goals. Unlike "purpose," goals are typically easy to find documented within an organization. Clearly developed goals are generally linked to clearly defined measurements. It's these measurements that can help link departmental tasks to greater organizational purpose and individual mission.

From grade school to college, the educational process is very individualized and the results are fully managed and credited to the individual. The "goals," in a large part, are a personal matter. And the measurements are most often grades.

In the workplace however, results and the resulting credit is a collective exercise. Should Gen^{m}s put boundaries on their passion and limit their individual thinking? Absolutely not. This will not serve the individual or the company. They should, however, view their career in steps and stages which will incrementally build towards that shared purpose which attracted them to the company in the first place.

Take the time to interview company leaders to understand how individual contribution and that of the immediate work group impacts the overall company. Follow a disciplined process to focus on the greater purpose:

- Understand the periodic (monthly, quarterly, and annual) measurements that determine success (in my department, division and company.)
- Link specific day-to-day activities to measurements you can impact.
- Monitor them and ensure they are consistent with your documented performance objectives.
- Capitalize on opportunities celebrate group success against key targets

You may have help, but then again, you may not

> *"[Gen^{m}s] should, however, view their career in steps and stages which will incrementally build towards that shared purpose which attracted them to the company in the first place."*

In an organization well-versed in managing Gen^{m}s, (like many reading this book) new hires will have a lot of help in this effort. In other environments this responsibility, again, will fall squarely on the shoulders of the new hire. By focusing on the critical link between purpose and individual contribution in a departmental/team environment, Gen^{m}s can keep the passion that sparks creativity without alienating themselves from the greater organization or experiencing personal frustration. It's this viewpoint that will help foster the political (yes, political) skills necessary to continue "up the ladder" of corporate success. Finding the personal mission in the company purpose can lead to the adventure of a lifetime — or at least a very successful career.

Thought Question: How do your goals align to the key company/department initiatives? For an exercise here, on one-half of a paper list your personal position objectives; on the other half, express the business objective(s) that your personal list aligns to. Does the matching make sense? Are there disconnects anywhere? If so, how might you adjust/remedy this?

Chapter 6 Highlights

The first real job represents a long awaited opportunity to impact the world in a new way – as a full fledged adult.

This group is worldly knowledgeable and they expect to be polled, listened to, and consulted upon entry into the business setting.

Making a difference in the world is important. Once you've identified at a high level with the company's purpose, view your career as incremental steps and stages towards achieving that vision.

In each task you approach, look for the link between the task and the "bigger picture" – company goals and mission statement.

Chapter 7
Charting Your Own Course

In previous chapters we've discussed the numerous ways that classroom learning differs from the on the job experience. Often the tools found in books aren't a direct fit to the practical realities of the "real world." However, there are some core fundamentals found in that Marketing 101 books that can help you with a life-long assignment — marketing yourself.

Positioning yourself among your competitive set isn't new. As a Gen^m, you are likely an expert at understanding the value of standing out in your crowd. However, as you move into your first post-college role, it's important to develop a plan...a very actionable plan for managing and monitoring the personal equity that you are now developing in business.

> *"You have a unique value proposition that can (and will) grow over time."*

Every good plan starts with a solid framework. Since you are "marketing" your talents, the tried and true marketing plan provides a great starting place for a structure:

Market Plan 101

    I. Current Marketing Situation
- *Relevant data on sales, costs, profits, the market, competitors, distribution and macro-environment*

    II. Opportunity and Issue Analysis
- *Identifies the main opportunities/ threats, strengths/ weaknesses, and issues facing the product line or company*

    III. Objectives
- *Defines the plan's financial & marketing goals in terms of sales volume, market share and profit*

    IV. Marketing Strategy
- *Presents the broad marketing approach that will be used to achieve the plan's objective*

V. Action Programs
- *Describes programs designed to achieve the business objectives*

VI. Projected ROI

Applying these topics to your career is easier than you think when you begin to view yourself as a valuable product in the marketplace. You have a unique value proposition that can (and will) grow over time. This can happen due to outside influences (macro-forces) or it can be driven by your own objectives.

Current Market Situation: Take a look at the competitive landscape

The first step in plotting your go-forward strategy is to clearly assess where you are today. Were you at the top of your class? Did you not only take advantage of the ever-popular "5 Year Senior" status, but pushed it into six or dare I even say a seven years? How well did you compete for this first job? Were you stressed by which offer to take or by which relative to leverage?

The good news is that the answers to these questions are only used to assess your starting point and key attributes of you (the product) today. Are you in a good competitive posture to get the things that you want next — the next promotion, the better client or case work, the next job with a new firm? What product attributes should you keep and which may need refining. The wonderful thing about graduation is that it begins a clean-slate for the future.

Opportunity and Issue Analysis: What am I facing?

Assessing the "Current Market Situation" is important when compared to the opportunities that it opens or limits you today. The Gen^m generation is better than those prior in listening to their own passion and determining an individual goal that is free from outside influences. Still, it's sometimes difficult to answer the question, "What do I want to do with my life?" at any age. It's, however, critical to identify near-term and long-term opportunities that can get you closer to success the way you (and only you) define it today. Of course, it will change over time and your "marketing plan" will need to be revised. Knowing that you will need revisions doesn't negate the need for a clear view of the opportunities that most interest you today, as this vision can provide you focus and clarity in planning your next steps.

> *"The Gen^m generation is better than those prior in listening to their own passion and determining an individual goal that is free from outside influences."*

Let's face it...We all have issues. Some of the "issues" become endearing character traits that define our personality. Others can get in the way of capitalizing on the opportunities that will help achieve long term goals. Taking a healthy (and honest) look at character traits and just plain bad habits can drive self improvement and increase the chance of future success.

Objectives: It's all up to you

The good news about the objectives in a post-college world is that you have complete control over them...The bad news about objectives in a post-college world is that you have complete control over them.

You can no longer depend on a syllabus expertly derived and neatly presented from your college professor that defines the objectives that lead to classroom success. Once you've determined the appealing opportunities for you, the next step is to define the objectives (hard goals) that will get you there and help you measure success. For some it can be expressed in terms of financial success or pay increases. Good news, these are easy to measure. For others, it may be to be in a position to help an important cause, like environmental concerns. These are more difficult to quantify, but can be qualified with specific timeframes and companies to help drive action.

Marketing Approach: Can you pitch yourself?

Now that you've assessed your characteristics (those positive as well as those under development), determined your opportunities, and supported them with clearly defined objectives, the next step is to "package" yourself. How are you going to market "you"? To those that are modest this may sound like an uncomfortable exercise in bragging. This is not the point.

What you need is a clear positioning strategy. How will you distinguish yourself in the competitive category to give yourself the best advantage? What is your approach to getting the recognition and advancement you deserve? There are several elements to consider:

- Playing Field: Are you in the right place for the next move? Are you surrounded by the individuals that can connect you to opportunity?
- Value Proposition: What value could you bring to the next opportunity? Can you articulate it clearly? If you met the hiring manager for your "dream job" could you communicate your value in an elevator ride?
- Differentiation: What makes you unique, special, different? How is this difference critical to success in the opportunity you seek?
- Reason to Believe: Why should someone believe your value proposition and claims of differentiation? What is your source of authority? More than in any other area, gathering the indisputable facts is critical. You should back your claims with hard examples of experience and measurable success that substantiates your position.

Action Programs: Get going!

So...what are you going to do to make these goals a reality? For some this is second nature and for others it's constant fight to stay on target. For either group it's important to document (yes we're back to report writing) the specific actions that you plan to take to achieve the objectives you set earlier. Remember, these have clear metrics and timelines so it's best to get started as quickly as possible. The following questions can help your thinking:

- What resources are available to help you? Do you have the money right now to take a graduate course or is that unrealistic at this time?
- How can you develop a realistic, yet aggressive plan that will get you where you want to go? What is the value of a plan that puts you significantly behind in the first phase?
- If the goal is far-reaching, are there milestones along the way that you can celebrate or reward yourself?
- How will you handle setbacks?

> *"Action is the only path to success, so ensure you are clear on how the actions will make your goals a reality."*

Projected Return: Only you know the pay off

To keep "focused on the prize" you'll need to continually assess the prize and its ultimate impact on your life. As previously stated, life and career goals are fluid. The young lawyer with an eye on being partner may reassess the impact to his or her personal life once that personal life includes others. The dream of traveling the world may seem less appealing after the first year of airline "platinum status."

This doesn't mean that the goals are not relevant, but they are only guideposts on the journey. The "return" on your career investment can be recalculated with the inevitable changes that life brings.

Thought Question: You have a weekend getaway planned with your girlfriend, and deposits have been made at the location site. On Friday afternoon your boss comes to see you in a panic. He needs all-hands-on-deck for a problem that's come up with a customer, and expects some recommendations by the team on Monday morning on how they might address and remedy the issue. What do you do?

CHAPTER 7 HIGHLIGHTS

Gen^{m}s need to learn to market themselves in order to obtain career growth.

Follow Marketing 101 guidelines to create your own brand. Consider the landscape, evaluate your competitive competencies, and create your action plan.

You- and you alone – are responsible for defining your objectives and achieving them.

Continually ask yourself how you want to be perceived in the marketplace and create your brand to achieve that result.

Keep your sights focused on your ultimate career goal(s).

Chapter 8
Where's the Bar?

You now have a strategy for migrating to the real world of business — complete with a plan to market the unique talents that make you a valuable contributor to "the greater good." Through your eyes, you'll see the good, the bad, and the ugly. You'll experience wonderful successes and disappointing failures. It's only natural. So, how do you know if "this is it?" Is this the place for you? Are you working toward a career goal that will ultimately lead where you want to go?

You now get to set your own bar

In college there are numerous opportunities to benchmark against a peer set with short-term goals that are very similar to yours — making the grade, receiving the scholarship, and getting the job offer. The "bar" of success is pretty easy to spot. Now, you are not only in charge of applying the self discipline to reach the bar, but you have to define it. In fact, you will keep defining it throughout your life. There are many 40-somethings still asking the question, "What do I want to be when I grow up?" and "Am I a success?" From now on you will need to determine if you are "on track" to reach a moving target.

> *"As you continue to plan, evaluate, and alter you career strategy, focus your personal bar on building skills that support your passion."*

Specific careers and the sequence of jobs will vary greatly and unforeseen obstacles and opportunities are guaranteed to alter even the best plan of attack. This does not mean, however, that career management is a complete "roll of the dice." As you continue to plan, evaluate, and alter you career strategy, focus your personal bar on building skills that support your passion…Yes, passion. While life may throw curve-balls and your career goals and jobs along the way may change, your core passions will remain relatively constant.

- What makes you excited about the job you are doing today?
- What motivates you to go the extra mile on projects?
- When you describe your profession to others, what is it that you highlight?

While these can be difficult questions to answer, they are essential to understanding your motivation. Ultimately, what do you really want from your career?

- How important is financial gain?
  - Is it a marker for achievement?
  - Is it simply a means to acquire life's necessities?
- Are your professional life and social life intertwined?
  - Is it important to work with people you like?
  - Are your personal values reflected in the job you have today?
- Where do you see yourself in five years…ten years?
  - How critical is your work to this vision?
  - Is work at the core of your image or an enabler?
- Where do you draw the line on work-life balance?
- What is your inventory of personal assets?
- What are some of the personal obstacles that should be considered?

"Ultimately, what do you really want from your career?"

Meet Emily

Emily is a twenty-four year old recent graduate from the University of Virginia. With a great college resume and engaging personality, Emily entertained several opportunities before accepting a job offer with The Coca-Cola Company in her home town of Atlanta. The first two years have been great. The corporate training program has Emily working with other new hires, as well as seasoned professionals in her selected field of marketing. Emily loves the company and being a part of the team. Emily believes in what the company and "her brand" are trying to do…she has to. If she doesn't believe in the vision, then the spark in her that drives hard work and creativity is gone. Friends no longer joke about selecting the competitor's product outside of work…it's not funny to Emily.

Financially, Emily is doing well. The steady bi-monthly check and solid benefits give Emily the ability to follow her favorite leisure activities:

dating and biking. Emily is very social and enjoys weekend trips with friends developed inside and outside of work.

Emily thrives in a company structure. She leverages both her passion and talent for working with and influencing others. Her goals are to continue to rise in the organization, but not at the expense of her life outside work. For Emily, work is best when collaborative and she is most proud of team and company accomplishments.

Meet Matthew

Matthew graduated from Georgia Tech with honors. While he went to school just blocks from where Emily now works, his passions and career vision couldn't be less similar. Matthew's "day job" is in development for a software firm based in Washington DC. This employment is a necessary step in getting to his real goal: to be a technology entrepreneur.

For Matthew the vision of success can be encapsulated into one image — his picture on the cover of Inc. Magazine. Although he is a good worker with solid contribution and a good performance rating, Matthew has no real loyalty for any company he didn't build. He works very long hours and is no stranger to "all nighters" to get a program complete.

This doesn't mean, however, that Matthew isn't social — quite the contrary. He and his two best friends from college are working together to get the beta version of their own anti-virus software completed. They set this goal years ago while passing the college-based "incubation center" on a daily basis. For Matthew, the goal is clear and no sacrifice is too great to make his company a reality.

Financially, he is also content. Like most Gen^{m}s money is a means to an end, not the end itself.

Matthew loves the challenge of an individual goal. Although he works with his small team, he firmly believes that he can change an industry. Look at the people that have done this successfully before him. Are they any smarter than he is? Not in Matthew's eyes.

Be your own bellwether

How can one formula for success serve these very different individuals? Clearly, there isn't a one-size-fits-all equation for measuring success.

The dictionary defines success as "the achievement of something desired, planned, or attempted." The key is to explore your personal talents, goals and desires. Unlike the structure provided in college, you will no longer be able to look to others for a relative benchmark. You can, however, look to mentors and to other successful individuals for insight into the types of decisions or actions that can help you plot your strategy. As you explore your success criteria further, consider the following questions:

- Who inspires you?
    - What about their life is attractive?
    - How do you think they achieved their goals?
- Who can you emulate?
- What groups can you join that attract people you would define as "successful?"
- How can you pattern key activities today after those who have achieved goals similar to yours?

Ultimately, success is a journey and will be measured by steps along the way. Enjoy the process and don't be afraid to regularly reevaluate your target — it will evolve over time.

Thought Question: You're part of a sales team rotational program that includes four learning segments. Each segment lasts around 6 months. You reach the third rotation segment and realize that you really don't like the type of work you've been asked to perform, nor the supervisor you're reporting to. What do you do?

Chapter 8 Highlights

Up until this point, the educational system had defined success for you. Now it's up to you to define success for yourself.

You will follow different paths and different goals than your classmates – and that's okay.

Ask yourself probing questions to determine your ultimate motivation and goals.

Seek out role models and mentors with who can help you achieve success.

Gap Odyssey – Section 2

Navigating the Business Highway - The Experienced Leader

Chapter 9
A Workforce Like Never Before

If you have managed people for several years, you have probably already noticed the differences between how your generation entered the workforce and how the Gen^{m}s are doing it. Predictability....gone. Loyalty.... lost. Commitment....depends on the day. These certainly aren't the Chevy buying days when dad decided a new car was needed, walked into the showroom with the exact car in mind, did a bit of price negotiating, and ultimately walked out in the 3rd, 4th or further generation Chevy in the family. Granted, back then there weren't the diverse alternatives of Lexus, BMW, Honda, Toyota, Kia and the like. While there were still choices back then, Pontiac, Cadillac, Oldsmobile, Buick, Ford, the loyal consumer rarely jumped from brand to brand. If grandpa had a Chevy, dad likely had a Chevy, and the next generation would be introduced to the Chevy brand as well.

Today, the youngest of workforce generations take the approach of not caring whether dad or his dad had a Chevy. Nope, this new generation goes directly to the brand of their vision regardless of prior family history, with dad cringing all the way.

The same goes for mom. The local supermarket was the haven of food delights. Mom would go weekly, fill up the cart with everything from the healthy veggies and fruits to all the sugary cereals and high cholesterol standards (ah, that Sunday morning bacon!). Today, the shopping experience in the new generation includes specialty stores for organics, high protein, and gourmet selections.

"For the seasoned manager, this is indeed a generation like never before."

Get ready for a different drum beat and a different march

This new generation does not rely on nor get impressed with history or protocol. Throw out the wall pictures of the company history, the group photos of the early sales, and the engraved plastic marketing pens. You can also do away with those drawer organizers and in and out boxes. For the Gen™s they'd prefer the iPod player (and headphones please), just the box of paperclips (no fancy cup necessary to store them in), that pretty flat screen monitor (plasma if you would) and a comfy ergonomically designed chair. Ok, thank you very much.

For the seasoned manager, this is indeed a generation like never before. Dentist appointment at 12:30 in the afternoon (ok, I'll be back the following morning); cute little niece has a cheerleader competition at 3pm (oh, gotta run); hubby has tickets to the evening ball game (well, adios at 4pm so I can get ready).

For the boomers, dad always walked in the door like clock-work at 6pm, mom was ready with dinner at 6:15pm, dishes were hand-washed by 7pm, and off to the small screen (not the iPhone or iPod) but yes, the TV, to gather around for the nightly news and maybe a sitcom or two.

The technology learning curve for the Gen™s is really just a slight bend

As manager, flexibility in style and approach is required to succeed in the current world of diversity. From a technology perspective this new generation will run circles around all before them. They love, cherish, and embrace new technology likes it's the latest and greatest action figure or beanie baby. Like the Rubik's cube, these bright new stars don't need instruction manuals or user guides. Nope, just let me charge the darn thing up, and then "give me space", cause baby, I got this figured out already. Moving screens, multiple overlays, eye popping pictures and visuals….all in a device that fits comfortably….in my pocket!

> *"From a technology perspective this new generation will run circles around all before them."*

Ever notice that this new generation struggles with creating PowerPoint presentations? From the manager perspective, they gaze and wonder "why can't this kid figure this out…god knows I can do this". The reality is that this generation already views PowerPoint as archaic. They've already been weaned on html, flash and the like, so now PowerPoint looks like ancient history with no point or purpose. You want a presentation? Hey let me stretch a bit here in my comfy work space and prepare that work of art in a format more dazzling and interactive for you.

Whether it's an iPod, iPhone, Wii, MacPro or Playstation, this generation lives and breathes for the next new, cool device to streamline their lives. As dad and granddad salivated over the new supercharged Mustang, Gen^{m}s have the date set and circled for the next generation technology device.

Whatever you do, keep it lively!

For the seasoned manager, this new group of eager youngsters requires ongoing stimulation and growth opportunities. Make no mistake, they hate boredom. Impose an environment of redundancy and monotony and you'll quickly lose the spirit of the young. But create a landscape based on open vision and the outcomes are boundless. The key is determining what can sustain that spark and twinkle over the extended period. I've assigned some cool, creative projects to new Gen^m stars. The projects historically have taken weeks, perhaps months to gain a grasp of and determine a sound course of direction. But today, as if you just turned the corner, these bright youngsters quickly have it figured out, and now they're ready and eager for the next hill to climb and conquer. Brainpower developed through a challenging and competitive college experience combined with latest and greatest technology tools and resources creates a powerful (almost intimidating) new generation genius that at times can be jaw-dropping to the seasoned leader.

> *"With the young Gen^m, talk, probe, and explore those things that ultimately bring that spark and twinkle to their eyes. Keep an open mind, challenge and invoke the creative spirit, and promote new horizons and you have a formula for sustained success."*

In today's diverse melting pot, it's critical to identify each young individual's "hot buttons", and manage accordingly to achieve maximum success. Identifying hot buttons means active engagement and commitment by the manager. Idleness or passivity just won't cut it. These are times to force the restraint of history, and alternatively create the mental white board that's clean, fresh and unscathed. With the young Gen^m, talk, probe, and explore those things that ultimately bring that spark and twinkle to their eyes. Keep an open mind, challenge and invoke the creative spirit, and promote new horizons and you have a formula for sustained success.

Those formula ingredients may balance differently for each individual, but rest assured that the ultimate blend and mixture still create similar outcomes. Success!

And the walls came tumbling down

To the extent of brick and mortar and the four walls within the company landscape, the Gen^m generation refrains from borders and boundaries, and that extends to their own personal work space. While airy and freshness are common denominators for this mass, they don't like the "friendly confines" of the cube environment. Rather, they prefer to establish their own balance of work setting, with the mindset that optimal work performance can be achieved whether that be in the office, at the local bistro, in the park, or at the coziness of home. This generation sees no value around formality of work setting protocol, and if given their preference would fill their internal company work space with décor to meet their own personal style and brand. This is a radical shift from the "let's take attendance" and "here's your name plate" mentality of prior generations. Flexibility and freedom is the name of the game. Mandate a firm work schedule that requires regular in-office appearance and you may drive some success over the short-term, but again make no mistake that within a reasonable period of time that bright, aspiring star will be gone, gone, gone for better horizons with a more progressive company and leadership team.

They'll want the cake and want to eat it too

This "workforce like never before" revolves around the mantra of work-life success. Unlike its predecessor "work life balance", this generation has figured out that success can be achieved without total balance. As life for them is typically spontaneous and fluid, "balance" is a panacea that has no merit because life is always in some state of flux on the longer continuum. They've seen the aging and strain of their parents through layoffs, excessive work schedules, extended business trips, divorces, community/world violence and death. They have no interest in mirroring that track, and assume and believe that they have a better mousetrap to "do it better". So the mid-day dentist appointment (didn't dentists back when work evening hours?), 3pm cheerleading competition, or the evening basketball game don't disturb the commitment-meter of this generation. They'll work smarter, faster, but in a flexible personal world that accomplishes all their areas of stimulation within a clock that just extends v. cycles.

> "This "workforce like never before" revolves around the mantra of work-life success. Unlike its predecessor "work life balance", this generation has figured out that success can be achieved without total balance."

In the manager context, this whole ensemble requires new wave thinking and behavior. Throw out the old (boomers), and bring in the new (Gen^{m}s). It's a whole new ballgame baby. Readjust your compass, embrace the oncoming (and ongoing) unknown, and ultimately seize the moment to bottle this new energy called youth and aspiration.

Thought Question: As a department manager you have a new project that requires some innovative thinking and thought process. In determining a "project plan" for this new initiative you need to determine both the "project lead" as well as other project team members. With a blend of both young hires and experienced staff members with 1-5 years of company experience, what factors will you use to craft the project team structure?

Chapter 9 Highlights

This new generation does not rely on nor get impressed with history or protocol.

Whether it's an iPod, iPhone, Wii, MacPro, or Playstation "x", this new generation lives and breathes for the next new cool device to streamline their lives.

If the manager can create a landscape based on open vision the outcomes are boundless. The key is determining what can sustain that employee spark and twinkle over the extended period.

Developed brainpower through a challenging and competitive college experience combined with latest and greatest technology tools and resources creates a powerful (almost intimidating) new generation genius that at times can be jaw-dropping to the seasoned leader.

Keep an open mind, challenge and invoke the creative spirit, and promote new horizons and you have a formula for sustained success.

Unlike its predecessor "work life balance", this generation has figured out that work-life success can be achieved without total balance.

Chapter 10
It's More than Just a Great GPA and SAT Score

For the business leader, team and culture dynamics all start with the identification and selection of human capital. As such the traditional recruiting and on-boarding methods likely won't yield the optimal results within the current workforce mix. For today's recruiting efforts to be successful, be prepared to invest more time, have more in-depth discussions, and get more deliberate with your overall process.

Not so long ago, recruiting was just a refined methodology to follow. You found some qualified candidates (at least based on the resume), did the traditional behavioral interviewing questioning, narrowed down the list to a more manageable number, included other internal members to the process, checked references, and extended the offer. All set. Perhaps a little bit of preparation in advance of the start date, but ultimately a pretty smooth deal as you wait until Day 1 when your eager new hire walks through the front door.

You provide the workspace, hopefully have a computer setup ready (what a novel thought), introduce your new member to others on the team, point out the restroom and break areas, perhaps join up for lunch, and then voila….everyone is off and running. If it was only still so simple!

It's a diverse candidate base in more ways than one

Today's hiring of young talent off the college campus has become quite complex. No longer does the GPA or SAT score provide the true and ultimate gauge of future success. Also, the blend of international students creates an additional mix of experiences and backgrounds never quite seen before. All told, while students have probably never been brighter, and our colleges never more rigorous in providing quality advanced education, what gets lost in the preparation is overall communication and fit.

> *"Overall, never has a group been more prepared academically though more unprepared to mentally and communicatively enter the real world."*

For many in this newest generation, the challenge isn't in achieving success in the classroom, but rather being able to relay that experience to the corporate context. Some resumes lack quality, substantive information with the student losing focus that the resume is the ante to enter the interview process with the prospective company. Beyond the resume, many of even the best and brightest fail to adequately prep for the interview, and are ultimately challenged with putting together meaningful sentences and paragraphs that ultimately need to reflect well on themselves. Overall, never has a group been more prepared academically though more unprepared to mentally and communicatively enter the real world.

Reach further to determine "fit"

For the hiring manager this means that the recruitment process must extend beyond the basics. The interview probe needs to drill down heavily into the student's ability to communicate thoughts, articulate how their academic achievements can transfer into the business setting, and describe what their personal motivators are (which in itself are dramatically different than the workplace generations that preceded). This becomes the essence of "fit".

> *"For the manager, you must invest more time, more inquisitiveness, and more probing to be sure that a candidate truly will fit on all dimensions of your search criteria."*

However the organization or manager may define it, "fit" goes beyond the grades. So here are a few questions to consider when probing for fit:

- How has your college experiences prepared you for your career aspirations?
- Why should our company hire you v. the number of other student candidates that applied for this position? What makes you unique?
- How would you define "company culture"? What are the components that make up an effective working culture? What would be your initial approach in acclimating within our culture?
- How would you define success, and how does that differ from the academic to the corporate landscape?
- Please provide an example of a school team project or initiative that didn't go 100% according to plan. What got sidetracked, and how did

- you and/or the team deal with this? What role did you play in the process? What did you learn from the experience?
- What tends to get you frustrated?
- If you look out both 1 year and 3 years from now, what do you think your life will look like?
- Describe a time when you went beyond the call of duty or expectations to get something done. What did the efforts look like, and what were the results? What did you learn from that experience?
- How competitive are you? How do you define "winning"? Is it ok to be #2 or #3 relative to competition?
- Let's take the example of you working on a project individually. It's a Friday, and everything is progressing well towards the final completion on Monday. You're feeling really great, with the goal line in sight. However, at 3pm your external project client calls, and states that they need some modifications to the initial project spec, but can't have the ultimate deadline extend beyond Monday based on an executive committee meeting that they have scheduled. What would you do?

While the answers themselves may be important to varying degrees based on your particular role or organization, most importantly is the thought process and articulation of such thought to the questions that will typically reflect whether the student candidate is a suitable "fit" for you and your company.

The take-away here is that historically traditional recruitment tactics won't work to best evaluate and assess today's student graduate. For the manager, you must invest more time, more inquisitiveness, and more probing to be sure that a candidate truly will fit on all dimensions of your search criteria. Much has been written about the cost of turnover, typically ranging anywhere from 1x to 5x the employee's annual salary. Whatever your calculation, bad hires result in bad and costly outcomes. Invest upfront to help increase your chances of new hire success.

Get on board with today's on-boarding

Let's say your new hire has made it through the recruitment process and is ready to embark on his/her entry into your department and organization. No longer is the half or full day general orientation process sufficient to get a new hire jumpstarted properly. Rather, for sustained results (both early stage as well as longer term), today's manager truly needs to invest as a steady mentoring influence.

> *"The ultimate goal is to provide a meaningful forum and process that helps a new hire succeed within the role and culture."*

There is a gray differential between the topics of mentoring and coaching relative to purpose, duration and process. Without splitting hairs, the ultimate goal is to provide a meaningful forum and process that helps a new hire succeed within the role and culture. Call it coach, mentor, counselor, it doesn't matter.

In the end, it's all about results. So from a manager perspective think about the following personal mentoring investment:

- Do you consistently invest meaningful time to meet with each of your employees for the purpose of their development?
- Do you demonstrate inclusive behavior that allows for each employee to be heard?
- Do you promote the exploration of needs, motivations, skills and thought processes that create a sustained roadmap for success?
- Are you accessible in dealing with the "unknown" when it arises?
- Do you effectively observe and listen, as well as ask "seek to understand" questions as appropriate?
- Is the development relationship truly collaborative v. one-sided directive?

Recruitment, on-boarding, coaching, mentoring....finding the right blended formula is ultimately the prescription for success between manager and employee.

Thought Question: Jeremy's been on your team for around a year as a college hire. He's doing a really great job, but you've noticed that over the last few months he's been bouncing inconsistent work hours, and looking a bit frayed on some mornings. Clearly Jeremy is burning the candle at both ends. What approach, if any, would you take in mentoring/coaching Jeremy?

Chapter 10 Highlights

Today's hiring of young talent off the college campus has become quite complex. No longer does the GPA or SAT score provide the true and ultimate gauge of future success.

For many in this newest generation, the challenge isn't in achieving success in the classroom, but rather being able to relay that experience to the corporate context.

For sustained results (both early stage as well as longer term), today's manager truly needs to invest as a steady mentoring influence.

Call it coach, mentor, counselor, it doesn't matter.

Chapter 11
Capitalize on Culture

Ok, you've done good work in the recruitment process, and have some bright Gen^{m}s joining your team. But the job as manager is still changing, still evolving, and includes more diverse and sustaining coaching and mentoring. Is it worth it?

The answer is simply "Yes"! This generation will have a positive impact on your company's culture. More than previous generations, this group truly cares about the impact of their work on the world and they want to be a part of something that is bigger and more important than they are. Greed doesn't always win the day. They are competitive, but compassionate. They are looking to leave a lasting mark on the world. They believe that previous generations have really messed things up and it's "on them" to fix it.

> *"More than previous generations, this group truly cares about the impact of their work on the world and they want to be a part of something that is bigger and more important than they are."*

Stand for something, and it better be good

This group doesn't feel "lucky to just have a job" like previous generations. They've grown-up during relative boom-times and despite some weaved-in fluctuating economic climates they remain positive. All their Facebook friends will know the reputation of the company they work for and the Gen^m hire cares that the public perception is positive. No one wants to apologize for something they do 40+ hours a week. They want to be part of a great company, and a great company culture.

For the business leader, being able to communicate on what your company stands for (on numerous dimensions) will provide the basis and foundation for your Gen^m employee community to embrace. As such, consider the following:

- What does your company stand for?
  - Can you articulate the company purpose clearly?
  - Does it have meaning beyond a functional description?
- What impact does your company make on the world?
  - How does it directly impact through its products and services?
  - What is its indirect impact on the community and environment?
- What values link your company community
  - Are there shared causes?
  - Are the values widespread and actively accepted and practiced by the leadership?

Once these elements are defined, it's important to communicate them. The Gen[m]s want to understand and impact the world around them. They will look for evidence that the company statements —from vision to purpose and mission — are not only words. They will watch to see if the leadership team, especially at the very top, truly "live" and exhibit the culture that is promoted.

Make no mistake that culture has more impact on morale and retention than meets the eye. Today's employees are a smart breed. Companies can talk a good game on culture, but savvy employees will quickly see through the smoke screen of idle pontificating if managers and leaders don't "walk the talk."

All told, culture is a powerful company component that defines the pulse of the business and the association of its employees. While words of mission and vision formalize the culture, it's the actual acts and behaviors, particularly at the leadership level, that defines what a company really stands for, demonstrates what they are passionate about, and exhibits whether they are true to the cause or are just smiling faces in a dark cavern.

Managers and leaders need to be genuine in representing culture. It's isn't about corporate cheerleading, though that can be of value as well. It's more about being true to the company's heart and soul, and showing a steady embrace of what makes your company great, both from the core deliverable and market/community reputation perspective.

Great cultures + great people = great outcomes!

Thought Question – Shannon's been on your team for around two years, and is a solid performer. Rumor has it that she's been casually exploring outside opportunities. You'd hate to lose her as she has a lot of potential for the organization. What would you do?

> ### CHAPTER 11 HIGHLIGHTS
>
> Gen^{m}s greatly care about the reputation of the company they work for. They are not just grateful to have a job; they want to work for an organization that is making a difference in the world.
>
> Make no mistake that culture has more impact on morale and retention than meets the eye.
>
> Culture is a powerful company component that defines the pulse of the business and the association of its employees.

Chapter 12
Communication Beyond the Four Walls

One of the most striking differences between Gen^{m}s and other generations is their copious communication style. Each business culture – and each generation within a culture – has a tacit understanding of how much communication is necessary and appropriate, similar to an understanding of how much personal space is appropriate.

No such thing as "TMI"

To the Gen^{m}s, there's really no such thing as TMI, or too much information. From "I just ordered eel and avocado sushi for lunch" to "I can't go to the gym today because I have some sort of foot infection…gross!!!" they put it all out there for the world to see. The rest of us are often baffled by this lack of filter between thought and speech – but understanding the reasons behind it can provide valuable insight.

The evolution of 24x7 collaboration

What we call technology advances are simply "the way it's always been" for the generation entering the workforce today. For most of their adolescence and adult life, they've had many communication vehicles at their disposal:

- Phone — cellular, of course
- Email — a bit slow, but good for talking with the older generation
- Text — complete with its own language
- Blogging — great for spreading your POV
- Twitter — in case someone needs to know exactly where you are and what you're doing
- Social Media Sites (MySpace/ Facebook)— Great for sharing your entire life – photos, events, plans – with your network of friends

Most of these communication vehicles have something in common: they are available (and easy to use) 24x7. Some of them, namely Twitter, even encourage 24x7 usage. With all these social/information forums at their disposal, it's no surprise that this generation is not shy at all about sharing their round-the-clock opinions and views on just about anything.

Furthermore, many of these mediums encourage widespread collaboration. Unlike phone and e-mail, where the conversation primarily goes two ways, Twitter and social media sites encourage people to collaborate and discuss everything from political opinions to which lunch spots are best.

"Who wouldn't want to know exactly what I think?!"

This generation grew up with parents that listened to them…*really* listened to them and gave their ideas value, even when they were quite young. They also began using cell phones and even social media in their pre-teen and adolescent years. By the time they were 11 or 12, the whole world could listen to them. Not only that, their whole world does listen to them. Their impressive number of online friends take an interest in every entry they post. All these factors add up to their undeniable conclusion that *everyone is interested in everything they have to say*.

> *"Gen^{m}s believe that everyone is interested in everything they have to say".*

Upside down, inside out communication

For the manager overseeing this workforce of social medium experts, "top-down" and "bottom-up" communication strategies just won't cut it. Gen^{m}s simply don't understand or believe in traditional boundaries of old; rather, they believe that everyone communicates because everyone's thoughts are valuable.

For the leader that's adhered to the same communication strategy for the past 10+ years, this may not be great news. But here's a silver lining: As employees, Gen^{m}s are very inclusive. They automatically respect and want to hear everyone's opinions. They use technology to help formulate and spread their ideas. Collaboration is king and they use technology to get a wide-range of inputs…and they expect the same from their manager.

> *"As employees, Gen^{m}s are very inclusive. They automatically respect and want to hear everyone's opinions."*

All this sharing of ideas has a positive influence on the way they work. Because they've always solicited and valued other's opinions, they can synthesize a lot of input quickly.

So what does this mean to you, the manager? In the realm of overall inclusion, consider these leadership ideas:

- Proactively and regularly solicit opinions on a variety of topics.
- Include your team in devising and implementing solutions.
- Communicate business objectives and give your team autonomy to determine both department and personal goals that are relevant to overall business objectives.
- Share the challenges that you and/or the organization are facing.

In the social context confidentiality needs to be explained

Case in point: "Family Talk"

For boomers like me, family discussions at the dinner table were assumed private. Growing up in the south, I was very familiar with "family talk" and knew it was strictly confidential. In fact, most conversations fell in this category: assumed private unless obviously trivial or otherwise noted as "OK to share."

Today couldn't be more different. The percentage of kids who dine with parents and siblings is dwindling, and when they do they are often texting and tweeting at the table – or updating Facebook and MySpace after they clear their plate.

This openness extends to the workplace. If a new employee has an experience at work, they'll likely consider it fair content to discuss with a very broad audience. Not only is it likely shared; it's likely to live online for what may seem like (and be) eternity. In today's workplace, it's best to have nothing to hide – because this generation doesn't believe in hiding anything.

Many Gen[m]s don't come equipped with the "internal filter" inherent in previous generations – the filter that helps determine whether or not to share information. If you manage an environment where there is confidential information, make no assumptions. Be very specific in your explanations of what you expect in terms of confidentiality. In addition, be prepared to defend your request. This generation isn't used to confidentiality and may interpret it as "hiding things." By taking the time to explain it, you can diffuse any apprehensions on their part. Plus, if they interpret confidentiality to mean the company is "hiding things," you may be inviting more attention than you intended.

> *"If you manage an environment where there is confidential information, make no assumptions."*

Bottom line, make no assumptions. Meet with your new employees and make sure they understand:

- The specific information the company deems confidential.
- The policies and impact of intentionally or unintentionally sharing confidential information.
- The difference between using social media for personal and business reasons.
- The policy on individuals who blog on behalf of the company.
- Public source information can be used by the press and they can be quoted.
- The company's Media Management Policy.

A more "grey area" on sharing information surrounds the image they develop by over-sharing personal information on social media sites. A YouTube video with highlights from a fraternity reunion may be fun to share with friends, but it may make an unintended and lasting impression on co-workers. Tread lightly in this area – have respect for the right of Gen^{m}s to express themselves, but view this as an opportunity to coach and counsel on the potential negative downstream effects. The social medium arena is evolving and expanding at an unbelievably rapid pace. For the leader who likely doesn't have the time, interest nor skill set to stay abreast on all the new available venues, it's important to nonetheless recognize that information travels across many paths and mediums not exclusive to the business environment.

Thought Question:

You have a wonderful group of young professionals on your department team, blended in with more tenured colleagues. As you "manage by walking around", you notice that your Gen^ms tend to be spending a noticeable amount of time texting and communicating externally on their non-company devices (e.g.- iPhone). While not necessarily impacting the performance basis of the group, the behaviors tend to stand out among the broader team. What, if anything, would you do?

CHAPTER 12 HIGHLIGHTS

The Gen^m population is used to sharing personal information and minute details with the masses. Doing this has taught them that the world is listening and is interested in all they have to say.

For the manager overseeing this workforce of social medium experts, "top-down" and "bottom-up" communication strategies just won't cut it. Gen^{m}s simply don't understand or believe in traditional boundaries of old; rather, they believe that everyone communicates because everyone's thoughts are valuable.

Confidentiality is somewhat of a foreign concept to the average Gen^m member. It's crucial to be specific and to make no assumptions when explaining the company's expectations with regards to confidentiality.

Chapter 13
Engagement, Commitment & Accountability

In times of economic flurry nerves frazzle, leaders unravel, and employees in general get swept up in the tsunami known as corporate chaos. With businesses focusing strictly on the bottom-line, keeping shareholders optimistic, and primarily staying away from anything that the market and media can view as unethical, unfathomable or just down right stupid, leaders have the tendency to neglect the most basic and important criteria for success....leading!

Masked behind the guise of "too busy", leaders scurry from one panic meeting to the next, arming for the worst news scenario, and hoping their name doesn't fall on the list of incompetence or failure within the next round of reduction considerations and assessments. Swept up in the current incessant mainstream of bad economic news, perhaps this may be as Dickens referenced "the worst of times", though certainly time and history will be the true barometer of such.

Under the corporate microscope of chaos, fear and paranoia, the workforce dynamics take a hit. Employees "run for the hills" hoping to somehow stay on the active working ranks, leaders seem bleary-eyed based on the hours and demands of deep internal and external inspection, and executives are all-consumed with company and personal survival and reputation. Within all this, communication failures persist among the layered masses, and attention to the fundamentals of business get pushed aside. All the corporate mission and vision statements don't mean a hill of beans in today's landscape. It's survive, or be gone!

Our actions speak louder than organizational taglines

"Employees are the key to our success" or "we value our employees" are just two examples of what all organizations (small to large) pride themselves on. Yet where most leaders continue to fail are on the three fundamental dimensions of leadership — engagement, commitment and accountability.

Engagement – the act of being participative, attentive and interactive with others in a business or social setting.

Commitment - The state of being bound emotionally or intellectually to a course of action or to another person or persons

Accountability - the principle that individuals, organizations, and the community are responsible for their actions. The notion that leaders of an organization are held responsible for improving employee achievement and should be rewarded or sanctioned based on such success or failure.

> *"Nothing destroys culture within the four walls of corporate America more than the neglect of these three fundamental dimensions."*

While these seem like common sense basics, truth be told the new generation of young professionals highlight this over and over again as missing within their management team; and on the leader side, they will tend to admit (whether with or without prodding) that this gets consistently compromised or neglected just based on the demands of the day. Nothing destroys culture within the four walls of corporate America more than the neglect of these three fundamental dimensions.

From the employee perspective, especially the young professional, the lack of management engagement sends a destructive and numbing message while leaving the corporate newbie lingering in the fog.

> *"Employees want to ultimately feel that their manager cares about them."*

All too often the comments from young professionals include:

- I don't know what's required/expected of me.
- I've never had a formal objective setting meeting.
- My manager is never available or is unapproachable.
- I don't know what success looks like.
- I'm bored.
- My manager gives me menial, unchallenging work.
- I can't tell whether I'm doing a good job or not.
- I didn't go to college to do this kind of basic work.

Engagement and commitment are meant to get you out there

Executives complain of the changing culture or lack of buzz/energy in the workplace. Yet when was the last time a key/prominent exec (yes you, Mr./Mrs. CEO/COO) was seen just walking around the corporate complex, saying hello to the general rank and file, asking how things are going, sitting in spontaneous small group settings (just to chat).

Or the COO who conducts regular leadership update meetings, and states how he *wants* to hold smaller group get-togethers to "get to know everyone a bit better" and gain their ideas. Great words, great intent, but nope, it just doesn't happen. But at least he goes to sleep at night feeling good that he "said the right thing."

Sometimes the best tends to come when the organization conducts their annual Employee Opinion Survey. Such great intentions....let's ask our employees what they think, and what we can do better. But when all is said and done, charts and trends are developed, benchmarks are evaluated against, yet at the end of the day, what truly changes?

> *"This is the time to inspire, engage, and just "get after it" with your employees."*

Such hollow efforts smack in the face of what true leadership is supposed to be. Leaders can hide behind the façade of business demands, customer issues, and stakeholder anxiety all they want. In the end, it's failure because the leader (all the way up through the bold top executive) could really care less about culture and the overall employee ranks. Nope, it's really around personal survival, incentive payouts, and stock option values.

In challenging economic times, this isn't the time to pronounce the state of the corporation, with bold intent, and then hide on the top floors of mahogany walls. This is the time to inspire, engage, and just "get after it" with your employees. If the employees are the cornerstone of the corporation, then the time is always right and appropriate to solicit new means and new forums to get employees together and spark new ideas.

Really open yourself to new and different ideas

Today's Gen^{m}s seek open mindedness and flexibility. For the seasoned manager open mindedness sometimes takes a back seat to "this is the way we've always done it, or the way the policy states." It's difficult at times to stretch beyond that mindset as it's so ingrained, and an easy and comfortable stance to take considering the stress and demands of the typical work day. However, never has a generation from the college campus been so equipped with the technology and knowledge to bring new creative thought processes and ingenuity to the corporate stage. Effective connection doesn't mean embracing every hair-brain idea brought forth; rather, it's about stimulating and encouraging new, fresh thinking into the equation of interaction. Fresh faces tend to bring new waves of analysis and efficiency that can have far-reaching positive implications, both direct and indirect, and both within and beyond the internal corporate structure. Seeking and encouraging creative thinking goes a long way in providing connection across the generations.

Success should be a common vision

Investment also includes defining with the team what success looks like. Too frequently managers fail to develop clear, concise, and agreed upon objectives with their employees, assuming that they'll "figure it out" on their own. Bad assumption. One of the most important early initiatives for the manager-employee relationship is to discuss, identify and subsequently formalize what constitutes success, impact and "winning" within the culture. Without clear, defined objectives the employee is essentially trying to hit a bulls-eye with a blindfold on. In that scenario the rest of the team needs to "look out!", as the variance of achievement or failure can be extreme, with broad consequences to the entire team, and organization. Effective objective/success setting also requires regular follow up sessions to gauge whether all is on-track v. veering off-course a bit. Jointly inspecting and recalibrating where necessary keeps everyone properly focused on the overall goal.

> *"One of the most important early initiatives for the manager-employee relationship is to discuss, identify and subsequently formalize what constitutes success, impact and "winning" within the culture."*

Place the carrot a little higher

Gen^{m}s also aspire and seek support for professional development and stretch opportunities. This tends to derive from the campus experience for continued and stimulated learning, so the more they can replicate that within the corporate setting the more fulfilled they tend to feel. Ideally, the manager-employee relationship continually explores avenues and resources to further broaden the mind that can drive enhanced impact and fulfillment within the role. New training, challenging projects, utilization of the latest technologies and the like will all create an aura that the manager (and organization) cares about the employee and is willing to (yes, again) invest in the near and longer term success and satisfaction of the team member.

Engagement and commitment won't break the mint

To the corporate leadership team, when was the last time you:

- Just walked around (let's say just 15 minutes a day), and said hello to your individual employees (preferably those you have no significant history or interaction with)?
- Sat down in the middle of a collaborative department work space, pulled up a chair, and just started chatting with a small group of employees?
- Spontaneously attended a department meeting, just entering to say hello and converse in casual conversation?
- Invited an individual or small group of employees to lunch, nothing fancy, but just spur of the moment?
- Stood at your building exit door at 5pm on Friday afternoon and thanked your employees for their efforts during the week, encouraging them to have a good weekend, and expressing that you're looking forward to seeing them back on Monday?
- Attended (or better yet) actively participated in a company event (e.g. – softball game or bowling team) and blended in with the group without a lot of fanfare?

Simple stuff, but yet so distant in the minds of the current leadership framework.

> *"The current diverse workplace creates opportunities for leaders to engage at exciting new levels."*

Current times dictate that leadership get after it.

- Communicate, communicate, communicate
- Seek new ideas and creative thought processes
- Provide consistent performance feedback
- Be a great coach and mentor
- Stimulate the minds of others, particularly your high potentials
- Create, reinforce and "live" your vision
- Promote inclusion, so everyone "has a voice"
- Acknowledge successes and examine/fix the deficiencies
- Show that you care about your employees, and mean it

Engage and commit and the leader is on the right track.

Bring personal accountability back

Finally, organizations need to hold leaders accountable for their engagement and commitment levels. No more excuses around time demands, "unique times", or unforeseen distractions. If an organization is true to its basic fabric, that of its employees, then leaders should ultimately be measured on the true impact and success across the board. And it should hit on both compensation and retention!

The current diverse workplace creates opportunities for leaders to engage at exciting new levels. Eagerness and creativity abounds within the generational masses; energy is waiting to be untapped and placed onto high impact project frontiers; and sincerity is prevalent in employees wanting to be part of the overall winning solution.

Engage

Commit

Be Accountable

And ultimately, WIN!

Thought Question:

You have a young employee on your team with three months tenure. Through recent conversation you find out that her brother passed away around a year ago, and that the anniversary of his passing is approaching. The employee in question is coming off a four-day extended weekend (based on a company holiday and added-on PTO day). It's now Monday morning, you open your Outlook email and notice you have a message from your employee (dated Sunday evening at 10:30p) indicating that she is saddened by the anniversary mark of her brother's passing, and with a few remote family members in town from the extended weekend they have decided to have a short memorial on Monday, and that subsequently she'll be taking Monday off as well. As the manager, what, if anything, would you do?

Chapter 13 Highlights

With businesses focusing strictly on the bottom-line, keeping shareholders optimistic, and primarily staying away from anything that the market and media can view as unethical, unfathomable or just down right stupid, leaders have the tendency to neglect the most basic and important criteria for success….leading!

All the corporate mission and vision statements don't mean a hill of beans in today's landscape. It's survival, or be gone!

Nothing destroys culture within the four walls of corporate America more than the neglect of the fundamental dimensions of engagement, commitment and accountability.

In challenging economic times, this isn't the time to pronounce the state of the corporation, with bold intent, and then hide on the top floors of mahogany walls. This is the time to inspire, engage, and just "get after it" with your employees.

If the employees are the cornerstone of the corporation, then the time is always ripe and appropriate to solicit new means and new forums to get employees together and spark new ideas.

If an organization is true to its basic fabric, that of its employees, then leaders should ultimately be measured on the true impact and success across the board. And it should hit on both compensation and retention!

Chapter 14
New Chapters, New Approaches, New Aspirations

Like most aspects in life, the ability to pursue and embrace change are central. Organizations evolve from startup thru emerging to mature growth phases, and then must continue to re-invent to maintain a lifeline on the corporate tightrope. In life, infancy through adulthood maturation also places a burden on the "what now" and "what next". How do you plan on building your legacy, and under what framework and context will that be achieved?

For the Gen^{m}s, the issue won't be brainpower or how to build the next innovative mousetrap. For them, it's a matter of style, approach, flexibility and adaptability within a creative construct. It's recognizing that book smarts and business smarts are usually two very different things, and that one without the other typically won't equal "total success". In such early stages, it's about listening, keenly observing the corporate surroundings, establishing key network relationships, and designing an initial career (and life) roadmap that is practical, perhaps a bit bold, and yet flexible for potential change and detour. Gen^{m}s will be students as well as teachers in the changing business landscape, and they will define a new pace as well as balance for the generations that follow.

For the current leader, the manner in which to build, motivate and sustain high performance teams has never been more challenging based on the differences in total generations within today's work environment. The willingness and ability to continually grasp new technologies that ultimately prompt new ways of conducting business will require an embrace of new wisdom, broader input, and quicker thinking. The relinquishing of the adage that "seniority has its privileges," will need to be replaced with a new leader mantra that "inclusion of all" is the only way to stay ahead of the game.

Like every generation, each will look back and view what was as slow, archaic, and sometimes even a bit ridiculous in the thinking. For the present, though, times will never be more perfect for the acceleration of new and exciting chapters of what will define success on so many diverse dimensions.

Enjoy the experience!

LaVergne, TN USA
07 December 2009

166104LV00005B/2/P